The Educator's Compass

A Weekly Lunch Time Bible Study
Curriculum

By

Oasis Focus Inc.

Copyright © 2019 by Oasis Focus Publishing

Oasis Focus Publishing

A Subsidiary of Oasis Focus Inc.

P.O. Box 2351

Keller, TX 76244

© 2019 ISBN: 9781074823030

Printed in the United States of America

AKJV

Scripture quotations are taken from the American King James Version (AKJV) public domain.

NKJV

Scripture quotations are taken from the New King James Version (NKJV) public domain.

KJV

Scripture quotations are taken from the King James Version (KJV) public domain.

NIV

Scripture quotations are taken from the New International Version (NIV) public domain.

First Printing: July 2019

Printed in the United States of America

Acknowledgements

The inspiration for writing this Educator's Compass came from many sources. The foundational source is our heartfelt gratitude to God - the Creator of the heavens and earth. To Him we acknowledge the inspiration He gave each contributing author to share messages from their own personal lives of who God has been to them and what He has done in and through them. Our heartfelt gratitude to our Savior and Lord - Jesus Christ for His Lordship. Our heartfelt gratitude to the Holy Spirit inspiring each contributing author to express the heart of God's character.

We also appreciate all our ministry friends and partners who provide wings for Oasis Focus Inc. to fly in accordance with its purpose and mission. This book is dedicated to all our public-school educators who strive daily to ensure our next generation of leaders receive quality education. We believe in their callings as educators; and duly support them in prayer, mentoring and coaching.

Finally, a heartfelt appreciation to all our contributing authors for their time and generosity in sharing the messages in this book. With faith-filled prayer we know this weekly lunch time Bible study will be a source of inspiration, encouragement and equipping for educators, because of the power in God's Word. To learn more about our contributing authors, read about them on the "Meet Our Authors" page.

Contributing Authors:

Dr. Feyi Obamehinti

Linda Reese, M.Ed.

Joyce Spears, M.Ed.

Tammy Wright, M.S.

Vicki Vaughn, M.Ed.

Camille Cueto, B.A.

For the Cause of Christ,

Dr. Johnson Obamehinti

President, Oasis Focus Inc.

Table of Contents

3rd Six Weeks Grading Period

4th Six Weeks Grading Period

5th Six Weeks Grading Period

Introduction

Our greatest assets in our public schools are teachers. The 2016 American Community Survey counted about 4.7 M teachers in the U.S. including preschool to postsecondary, special ed and other teachers and instructors. Anyone that has taught school knows firsthand the workload teachers carry daily. In addition to their workload, many teachers have families of their own just like the rest of us. Because teaching is a draining type of occupation, we designed this weekly lunch time Bible Study for teachers to refuel and recharge around the word of God.

Teachers have 30 minutes lunch daily that many times they spend at their desk grading papers, sending emails or making phone calls home to parents. Their lunch time is not meant for official duties, but teachers still use this time for that. To equip and empower educators with the Word of God, we want them to make their lunch time a priority to nurture their spirits and souls.

This **Educator's Compass** has been specifically designed for lunch time fellowship. In a similar way that a compass is an instrument used for navigation and orientation, we at Oasis Focus Inc. have prayerfully designed this Bible Study curriculum to provide weekly spiritual navigation and orientation for public school educators. It is our prayer that through these weekly short 15 minutes study, teachers will receive spiritual nourishment, encouragement and community with each other. We encourage you to use a journal along with this study. Record your journey.

This is a charity project. It is our way of investing in our public schools' greatest assets-*teachers.* We welcome your donation to get this curriculum into every public school across the nation. Together, we can provide weekly spiritual fuel for our teachers. Check donations can be made out to: **Oasis Focus Inc.** and mailed to:

P.O. Box 2351

Keller, TX 76244.

All donations are tax deductible. Oasis Focus Inc. EIN number is: 45-3652658

All Scripture quotations, unless otherwise indicated, are taken from the New International Version (NIV).

The Word of God is a compass; providing direction and guidance to navigate life successfully.

Psalm 119:133 "Direct my footsteps according to your Word; let no sin rule over me."

Psalm 119: 105 "Your word is a lamp for my feet, a light on my path."

Psalm 119: 130 "The unfolding of your words gives light; it gives understanding to the simple."

Romans 15:4 "For everything that was written in the past was written to teach us, so that through the endurance taught in the scriptures and the encouragement they provide we might have hope."

Educator's Compass Bible Study Model

The *Hear-Believe-Apply* model is a systematic way of receiving encouragement from the word of God. Educators will not only read scripture passages from the Bible, but through reflective activation, their faith will be activated into action to implement the wisdom or principle in the selected scripture passage. It is our prayer that this systematic model of Bible study will help our educators grow in their walk with God because we were created for intimacy with God.

Hear: This is typically a scripture verse for the week's study. Our faith in God is built up when we hear the word of God. Romans 10:17 states that, "So then faith cometh by hearing, and hearing by the word of God." By reading and reflecting on the scriptures in each weekly lesson, faith in God's character will be stirred and built.

Believe: This is where the scripture verse for the week is explained using stories. After hearing the word of God, our faith is then activated. We believe and unlock the promises of God to receive the treasures packed in the scriptures. In Genesis 15:6, we see a picture of how Abram heard from God and then believed Him. "And he believed in the LORD; and he counted it to him for righteousness." In this scripture we see that Abram had heard the word of God in a vision (verse 1). What he heard stirred and activated his faith to believe God. The word Abram heard helped to activate his faith, that, in turn, unlocked the promises of God he heard in the vision. Another scripture from the New Testament also points to the importance of activating our faith as a precursor to believing God. Romans 15:13 states that, "Now the God of hope fill you with all joy and peace in believing, that ye may abound in hope, through the power of the Holy Ghost." Activating our faith to believe the promises of God for our lives causes us to abound in hope that God is faithful to fulfill His word.

Apply: This is where we apply the scripture verse for the week. Once we believe the word of God we heard, an action step is then required to implement the wisdom or principle in that word. God's word is truth for whatever circumstances we may be dealing with. Truth applied is what produces fruit in our walk with God. Truth applied, brings victory.

Between hearing and believing is a time of exploration. This exploration helps us understand the context of the scripture, the meaning of any principle associated with the scripture and what the text or principle reveals about God. Similarly, between believing and application is a time of discovery. This discovery involves reflection and prayer that helps us to receive a clear understanding of how the associated principle in the scripture works and its application to our lives. **The Educator's Compass Bible Study** is a working lunch study that should not take more than 15 minutes per day. We have made it easy to use; just follow the format.

Topic: Speak it into Existence

Hear: Genesis 1:1 "In the beginning God created the heavens and the earth."

Believe: A new school year brings with its new adventures and excitement. Imagine, you were part of the team when Genesis 1:1 happened. From absolutely nothing, God speaks, and then things begin to appear in heaven and on earth. As a Christian, you have that same power of the Holy Spirit to **speak things into existence**. This is called "faith."

Application: What are some things you would like to see happen this school year?

For you?

For your family?

For your students?

For your colleagues?

For your campus?

For your district?

For your community?

Write them down in your journal. Now take each of those things you have written down and **"speak"** them into existence in **prayer**. Take each of the things written down to God in prayer. You can speak into existence this new school year. Though, you don't know everything that will happen this school year, God does, and you can commit this new school year into His care. Close out your prayer time with thanksgiving. As God begins to answer each of your requests, be sure to share the testimony with your compass group. It is always an encouragement to others when we share answers to prayers.

Discussion Point: Briefly share with each other how faith is related to prayer.

Closing Prayer: Heavenly Father, thank you for this new school year. I commit my life, my calling and my desires for this school year into your hands. I trust you to make all things work together for my good and for my students, campus and district.

Topic: Increase

Hear: Job 8:7 "Though your beginning was insignificant, yet your end will increase greatly."

Believe: As educators, we sometimes feel inadequate with all the demands of a new school year. With new district and state mandates to implement, new programs, and new students that we are eager to get to know, a new school year might make us feel inadequate and sometimes insignificant. In this Job 8:7 scripture, Bildad (one of Job's friends) though not at first encouraging, gave an inspiring advise that gave Job hope that all be well. As a Christian, there is hope that you will have **increase** this school year, despite what might seem like insurmountable obstacles.

Application: What are some new mandates you are faced with this school year?

What are some new instructional programs you are required to implement this year?

Do you have new students in your class this year?

What are some challenges in your own family this school year?

Do you feel inadequate?

These are all valid feelings for an educator at the beginning of a new school year. As you answer these questions in your journal, receive encouragement from this week's scripture. Despite all these challenges, take courage in knowing that God is with you. God is for you. God is in you. God did not bring you this far, to abandon you. Your end will increase not just a little bit, but greatly. Again, you can have faith in God's faithfulness. As you pray, ask God to increase you greatly. Ask Him to help you meet and exceed all the challenges ahead this school year. Ask God to guide you and empower you to do your part and to do it well for His glory.

Discussion Point: Briefly share some of this new school year's challenges with your compass colleagues and take those to God in prayer together.

Closing Prayer: Heavenly Father, thank you for your faithfulness that You keep covenant and steadfast love with those who love You and keep Your commandments. We turn all these challenges and cares of this new school year into Your powerful hand and trust Your care for us.

1st Six Weeks Grading Period: Week 3

Topic: Confidence

Hear: Philippians 1:6 "For I am confident of this very thing, that He who began a good work in you will perfect it until the day of Christ Jesus."

Believe: Our American culture prides itself with consumer confidence; an economic indicator that measures the level of confidence consumers feel about the state of the economy and their personal financial situation. In this week's scripture verse, Apostle Paul assures the Philippians about his confidence in the faithfulness of God. Whatever God starts, He finishes. As Christian educators, we might not have all the details of how the school year will go, however, we can rely confidently on the unwavering faithfulness of God. God began a good work in you and that same God will complete what He started in you. This is where our confidence lies - in God's faithfulness, in God's power and in God's track record.

Application: Where do you need God's assurance and affirmation this week?

Is it in your personal life?

Is it in your family?

Is it in your classroom with some of your students who need extra assistance?

Is it with your some of your parents on how to get them on board with the new initiatives?

Is it with your colleagues?

Is it with your workload that seems to grow with each passing day?

Is it the mounting pressure of scaffolding instruction for your students?

Is it the upcoming school activity you have been assigned to lead?

Discussion Point: Briefly share some of the areas you need God's assurance and affirmation this week with your compass colleagues. Now ask God in prayer for the courage and strength to continue to do a good work this school year.

Closing Prayer: Abba Father, thank you for the assurance your word gives me today, that the good work you have begun in me, you will perfect until the day of Christ Jesus.

Topic: Hand of God

Hear: Nehemiah 2:18 "I told them how the hand of my God had been favorable to me and also about the king's words which he had spoken to me. Then they said, "Let us arise and build." so they put their hands to the good work."

Believe: Nehemiah was cupbearer to the king of Persia in 445 BC. He had received the news that the remnant of Jews in Judah were suffering and that the walls of Jerusalem were broken down. Nehemiah's compassion about the situation, moved him into action. He asked the king for permission to return and rebuild the city. The king granted his request. In this week's scripture, Nehemiah visited Jerusalem to see the ruins he had learned about. Nehemiah then went on to share with the officials guarding the ruins, how he got there. Because of the hand of God, Nehemiah received favor both from God and the king. The hand of God is symbolic of the power of God. Miracles happen because of the hand of God. Miracles are remarkable occurrences that cannot be explained with human intellect. The good news is, as Christians we can ask God for a miracle for whatever impossible circumstances we are facing. Only the hand of God can do the impossible on our behalf.

Application: What impossible situation(s) are you facing this week?

In your personal life?

In your family life?

At your school?

No matter the situation, God can be fully trusted. He is a master at performing miracles.

Discussion Point: If you are at liberty, briefly share one or two of the impossible situations you are facing with your compass colleagues. Encourage each other as you pray together.

Closing Prayer: Heavenly Father, we are grateful for your loving kindness towards us. We are resting on your character that you can be fully trusted with all our impossibilities. Just like Nehemiah, we will live to proclaim the greatness of your hand in our lives.

1st Six Weeks Grading Period: Week 5

Topic: Community

Scar: Hebrews 3:14 "We have come to share in Christ, if indeed we hold our original conviction firmly to the very end."

Believe: School provides a sense of community. A place of shared interest and mission. Each classroom is a community of learners that share experiences together. Hebrews Chapter 3 begins with a general encouragement to Christians who are in community together. Jesus Christ our Savior and Lord and following Him together helps strengthen our faith. Our work as educators is not an isolation sport. It requires community 24/7. Yet, our educational system has created an isolation culture that sometimes makes it challenging to have community. This is the reason, why many new teachers struggle their first year of teaching. They feel isolated. They feel as if no one understands what they are facing. This week's scripture enlightens us that as Christians, our **community** is based on our Lord Savior, Jesus Christ. As we settle into the new school year, it is important to make community a priority. This compass Bible Study is meant to help achieve that very goal of building a sense of community and camaraderie on your campus. You are not alone. There are other Christians who understand you and are rooting for you and your students to succeed this school year. Determine not to go at it alone this school year. You have your brothers and sisters in Christ with you.

Application: What are some things that give you a sense of community?

At home? At church?

In your classroom?

On your campus?

Within your district?

Discussion Point: Briefly share these things that give you a sense of community. Pay attention to what your colleagues have shared and take note where you have mutual interests besides school. Determine to build and grow together in these areas of interest this school year.

Closing Prayer: Thank you Jesus, for your sacrifice on the cross to make us a community of believers. Help us to develop and grow our community here on this campus this school year.

17

1st Six Weeks Grading Period: Week 6

Topic: Celebration

Hear: Ecclesiastes 3:13 "And also that every man should eat and drink, and enjoy the good of all his labor, it is the gift of God."

Believe: We all love a good time and commemorating special life milestones and accomplishments like birthdays, weddings, or graduations. While none of these are happening this week on your campus; it is still cause for celebration. It is the end of the first six weeks grading period! You and your students have braced through some challenging times. From acclimating your new students to your classroom and campus, to engaging parents as partners for the school year, you survived it all. Since the beginning of the school year, you have planned, written and documented at least thirty lesson plans. By now, your students are familiar with your classroom rules and procedures and your class starting to feel like a family. You have been hard at work, working late and arriving early to school. You have established a strong foundation for the school year. So it is time to celebrate! The scripture this week acknowledges the need for celebration after a time or season of hard work. Our scripture verse states the result of your hard work is a gift of God. Whenever you invest any amount of energy, effort, or passion to do something, and it yields a good result, you should celebrate. We have been conditioned by our American culture, to only see success as an end result. However, success is also recognizing the small steps completed during the process of achieving any goal. So today, celebrate! Celebrate your passion to teach. Celebrate your students and all the progress they have made so far. Celebrate your colleagues. Celebrate life. Celebrate you.

Application: What are some things you need to celebrate this week?

From your personal life?

From your students?

From your campus and district?

Discussion Point: Celebrate each other. Share your highs from your life, family, students, community etc. Fill your passion and motivation tank with these celebrations.

Closing Prayer: We are a grateful people. Thank you, Lord for how far you have brought us and helped us. We acknowledge that You are the wind beneath our wings. You are the One that has called us to teach. As we continue our year, empower us to be all we need to be, for your glory.

2nd Six Weeks Grading Period: Week 1

Topic: Light

Hear: Matthew 5:14 "You are the light of the world. A town built on a hill cannot be hidden."

Believe: Light is powerful. Imagine staying at a hotel that uses energy saving technology to turn lights on and off. By simply inserting and removing the room key, you can control the amount of light in the room. Unlike sound waves that are carried by vibrations through a medium, light does not require a medium for it to travel. The speed that light travels is an indication of the effect of light that ambassadors of Jesus Christ carry with them. Light is a form of energy. Light makes things visible. Light alters an atmosphere. Light guides. Light always has a source. The most important takeaway is that without a source, light will be incapable of its various effects. For ambassadors of Jesus Christ, we must also be plugged into the source of life to stay charged up to disseminate darkness. With one grading period under your belt, you can see different ways that your light is shining in your students' lives. The scripture this week, makes a bold declaration on how we must live as Christ's ambassadors. We are "lights" and we must be effective. We must shine. The world is counting on our light to help guide them into purpose. You are a light and must continue to shine!

Application: What are some ways that your light is shining?

In your personal life?

In your family?

At your school?

In your classroom?

Discussion Point: Briefly share with each other how your lights are shining for the Lord. Give God praise for all the ways He is working in each of your compass colleagues. Let your lights shine for Jesus Christ our Lord and Savior.

Closing Prayer: Heavenly Father, thank you for sending your son Jesus Christ to pay the ultimate sacrifice for our salvation. This sacrifice is what qualifies us as your light bearers. Help our lights to shine day by day for your glory in all we do and say.

2nd Six Weeks Grading Period: Week 2

Topic: Refuge

Hear: Psalm 46:1 "God is our refuge and strength, an ever-present help in trouble."

Believe: The medieval times are well-known for their fortified moats. These ancient buildings provided shelter and defense for people who were under attack or threatened by war or danger. The buildings were castle-like in nature, with huge doors and high walls. Though many of these buildings were built hundreds of years ago, some can still be found all over Europe and the Middle East. This week's scripture paints a picture for us. Our God the Creator of the heavens and the earth is a refuge. He is strong and can never be defeated in any battle or war. Whatever the attack; be it spiritual or physical we can count on our God's protection and defense. Additionally, we can count on His everlasting strength to carry us through times of difficulty. The best part of God's safety is that He is always available. He is never asleep or on vacation. He is an ever-present help in trouble. He is the best person to call upon when in trouble or distress. As the school year unfolds, many unforeseen challenges are unfolding with it. At this point, we are asking ourselves and each other, "Is it Thanksgiving or Christmas break yet?" It is during times like this that we need to rely on the help of our God. He is our fortified shelter. We can call upon the Lord for strength. We are not defenseless. We have a shelter. We have hope. We have an anchor.

Application: What are you facing today that needs the ever-present help of God?

In your personal life?

In your family?

At your school?

In your classroom?

Discussion Point: If you are at liberty, briefly share one area that you need the ever-present help of God with your compass colleagues. Now take those needs before God in prayer. He is Present.

Closing Prayer: Thank you Lord, that You are a solid refuge, a trusted shelter, a bulwark of strength, and Omnipresent. We cast all our needs on you and ask for your help in our situations.

Topic: Strength

Hear: Ephesians 6:10 "Finally, be strong in the Lord and in His mighty power."

Believe: Popeye the Sailor was an all-time favorite family cartoon in the 1960s. Through the years, Popeye has also appeared in comic books and arcade and video games. This fictional character was created by Elzie C. Segar. Popeye was known for his extraordinary strength which he got from eating spinach. His strength allowed him to accomplish incredible physical feats, often defeating the antagonist in the story. Popeye was always seen using his extraordinary strength to rescue others in distress. Ephesians Chapter 6 opens with admonition to different groups of people; children, fathers, servants and masters. After these greetings, the Apostle Paul gives a command. He starts with the word "finally" to communicate the last thought in his series of related admonitions. Paul commands that as followers of Jesus Christ, we must be strong; however not in our strength or our roles. We must be strong in the Lord only and in His mighty power. The Lord's power is enormous. The Lord's power is unparalleled. The Lord's power is transformational. The Lord's power is restorative. The Lord's power is healing. This is the kind of power we are encouraged to be strong in. As the instructional pressure mounts, and the classroom discipline problems arise, you can find strength in the Lord, your Savior, Father, Master, Friend, Counselor, and Advocate. Yes, you can find strength in the Lord, He never runs out of it.

Application: Who or what seems to sap your strength lately?

Is it a specific student?

Is it a demanding parent?

Is it a new assignment?

Is it the new district mandate?

Discussion Point: There is no shame in sharing our areas of need or weakness. Discuss with each other how this week's lesson is applicable to you. As a follow-up, journal your reflections.

Closing Prayer: Dear Lord, we come boldly to the throne of grace to ask for strength in this time of our weakness. Lord, we ask that we sense your nearness in a new way. May Your strength be perfected in us as we trust you with these areas that sap our strength. We thank you in advance.

Topic: Courage

Hear: Joshua 1:9 "Have I not commanded you? Be strong and courageous. Do not be afraid; do not be discouraged, for the Lord your God will be with you wherever you go."

Believe: One of America's sports icons is Jackie Robinson - a man of courage in a time that tested the culture of a society. Jackie Robinson was the first African-American to play baseball in the Major Leagues. Jackie demonstrated great courage during a time in American society when it was unacceptable for African-Americans to play professional baseball. In 1946, Jackie broke that racial barrier. He stood firm against discrimination and racism even when he received constant death threats. Jackie refused to allow those things to put fear in him or discourage him. Instead, he had a determined resolve that encouraged and emboldened him. In return for his determination, he earned the respect and support of many who believed it was time for America to finally have equal rights for all in sports. For his courage and contribution to baseball, Jackie Robinson was inducted into the Baseball Hall of Fame in 1962. Additionally, his jersey #42 was retired permanently as a symbol of honor. In this week's scripture, we see the young leader Joshua about to embark on his life journey, leading the Israelites to cross the Jordan River into the land God had given them. The journey required courage, lots of it; just as leading the Israelites who had a reputation for being rebellious and stuck in their ways. Moses, their deceased leader had led the Israelites to this point. Now, it was Joshua's turn to take the baton and lead the way into the promised land. God Himself, through His admonition put courage into Joshua, commanding him to be strong and courageous. God promises to be with Joshua all the way through the journey into the promised land and beyond. What an encouragement for educators walking in their calling as Christ's ambassadors. God Himself, has promised to be with you all the way through this school year and beyond.

Application: Is there anything putting fear in you? Honestly answer this question with at least one compass colleague.

Discussion Point: Fear is destabilizing. Faith, on the other hand, is empowering. How has your faith been stirred towards believing God? Share out loud and discuss with your colleagues.

Closing Prayer: Faithful God, thank you for your encouraging word not to be afraid or discouraged. We re-affirm our trust in You, and your command to be with us not only this school year but beyond. We declare our faith in You. We declare our hope in You. We declare our love in You.

Topic: Redeemed

Hear: Galatians 3:13 "Christ redeemed us from the curse of the law by becoming a curse for us- for it is written, "Cursed is everyone who is hanged on a tree.""

Believe: Ric O'Barry is 79 years old. In his early years, Ric trained dolphins and whales for the 1960s TV series *Flipper*. After training dolphins for ten years, Ric transitioned to advocating against industries that keep dolphins in captivity. What a huge contrast from someone who used to train dolphins for a living! Ric set out on a new path after having a deep personal reflection on the cruelty of abusing dolphins and whales for human entertainment. He founded the Dolphin Project to rescue and rehabilitate dolphins around the world. Ric O'Barry successfully reclaimed the value of dolphins from being a means of entertainment to valuing their intelligence as part of creation. Ric can be said to be a "redeemer" of dolphins. Jesus Christ did the same for humanity. He is our redeemer. His death on the cross was payment for our sins and eternal separation from God. Jesus Christ became cursed for us, so that He could redeem us from the curse of the law. We were guilty and Jesus' sacrifice on the cross paid our ransom. Jesus' sacrifice bought us back and gave us access to the Heavenly Father - an access that was lost originally in the Garden of Eden by Adam and Eve. Now, everyone that accepts Jesus Christ as Savior and Lord has the seal of redemption. Hallelujah to the Lamb! We are redeemed! Educators share this redeeming quality of our Savior. From advocating for students to standing up for injustices, educators are some of the best advocates. As followers of Jesus Christ, our faith in Christ requires and empowers us to speak up and advocate for those that cannot speak up for themselves.

Application: What is the Holy Spirit saying to you through this week's study?

Discussion Point: Take some time and share with your compass colleagues what the Holy Spirit is speaking to your heart. Pray for each other.

Closing Prayer: Heavenly Father, thank you for the salvation of our souls. Jesus, thank you for taking our place on the cross. Holy Spirit, thank you for speaking truth to our hearts today. Our one thing, is that you will be glorified in and through our lives. For this, we live, move and have our beings. Holy Spirit, fill us afresh with your power, inspiration, courage, and resolve to be the hands and feet of Jesus Christ – our Lord and Savior.

Topic: Unique

Hear: Psalm 139: 14 "I praise you, for I am fearfully and wonderfully made. Wonderful are your works; my soul knows it very well."

Believe: When the movie *Happy Feet* came out in 2006, it stole the hearts of both young and old. Mumble, the main character of the movie, taught us all about the beauty of uniqueness. In a community where having a singing voice is the norm, Mumble finds out he doesn't have a "heart song" (a unique song to attract a mate) like the other penguins. Instead, Mumble has a rare talent that the other penguins didn't have - tap dancing. Through a series of events marked with ridicule, rejection and disapproval from family and friends alike, Mumble comes to accept himself. He embraces his uniqueness, revels in being true to himself and changes his community for the better. This week's scripture verse highlights the truth of uniqueness. God in His intelligent design has created and wired each one of us for a unique purpose. As educators, we recognize the students that feel out of place in our classrooms or campus. Students that feel they don't belong, because they aren't part of the "cool kids" group. Students, just like Mumble, who are yet to discover who they are. The good news is God knew these students would be here on your campus and in your classroom. God knew these students would come into contact with you - a child of God. And through you, and your daily ministry in your classroom and your campus, these students will come to accept themselves and their uniqueness. The anointing of God on your life, helps call out the identity of these students. Through your words and actions, these students will embrace their "fearfully and wonderfully made" design. For such a time as this, God has brought these students to you so that they may know how God has made them unique.

Application: In what way(s) has God made you unique?

In what way(s) has God made your students unique?

In what way(s) has God made your colleagues unique? Your family unique?

Discussion Point: Briefly share with each other your uniqueness. Now, celebrate this uniqueness that expresses the beauty of our God. As you learn how to celebrate who you are, it becomes second nature to celebrate who God has created each of your students to be as well.

Closing Prayer: Heavenly Father, thank you for making us heirs of your kingdom through Christ Jesus our Lord. Help us to walk out our inheritance as sons and daughters of your kingdom.

Topic: Helper

Hear: John 14:16 "I will ask the Father, and He will give you another Helper, who will stay with you forever."

Believe: Christmas time in America ushers in a time of giving and outreach to those in our communities that need to see a demonstration of God's love through humanity. Many cities across the nation employ the assistance of Santa's Helpers to accomplish this joyous feat. Santa's Helpers are typically people in different organizations or families that take on the task of elves; gathering toys for children and food items for families. The elves are indicative of elves that live with Santa Claus at the North Pole and help make toys that Santa distributes to those children on his "nice list." This week's scripture points us to a Helper promised to every child of God. This Helper is the third Person of the Holy Trinity - the Holy Spirit. Jesus Christ promised us a Helper that will always stay with us. This Helper ensures we are successful in what God has called and assigned us to do. The Holy Spirit is the only Person that knows each student in our classroom. With this divine discernment, the Holy Spirit can guide us in our communication with students and parents alike. He can give us creative ideas on how to deliver a difficult lesson. Because the Holy Spirit is God, we can trust His guidance. His help is readily available and all we have to do is ask Him for whatever we need help with; in our lives, students' lives, or the task of teaching. This Helper is with you always and loves to help!

Application: What do you currently need the Holy Spirit to help you with?

Is it to plan lessons creatively in a way students' will quickly understand the concepts?

Is it in how to deliver instruction in a way that targets students' maximum learning style?

Discussion Point: Briefly share with each other what you currently need help with. This could be the current challenge with a student, parent or lesson concept. Now spend some time to pray for each other, asking the help of the Holy Spirit. Commit to Him and invite Him into the challenges.

Closing Prayer: Heavenly Father, thank you for making us heirs of your kingdom through Christ Jesus our Lord. Help us to walk out our inheritance as sons and daughters of your kingdom.

Topic: Unity

Hear: Psalm 133:1 "Behold, how good and pleasant it is when brothers dwell in unity!"

Believe: Ric O'Barry is 79 years old. In his early years, Ric trained dolphins and whales for the 1960s TV series *Flipper*. The dolphin, Flipper, was depicted first by a female dolphin named Susie then by another female dolphin named Kathy and subsequently by other female dolphins named Patty, Scotty and Squirt, respectively. These five dolphins became part of a community to ensure the success of the *Flipper* TV show. Sometimes the dolphins passed as identical "Flipper." This type of synergy is what happens when there is unity. Our scripture verse points to the fact that great things happen when there is unity. To dwell together in unity requires a sense of community. It requires having the same mindset on something. This is what we want to see in our classrooms. A community of learners that share a love of learning and are actively engaged in learning from one another. To achieve this type of unity, requires dedication, focus and determination. A unified classroom means, we have standard procedures that have been duly communicated and demonstrated to students. As the leader in the classroom, we get the opportunity to set high expectations for all students in other to create a synergy of instructional excellence.

Application: How would you rate your classroom management system?
Do all students know what is expected of them daily?
Do all students know what to do in specific situations?
- Such as in a fire drill?
- Such as in a lockdown?
- Such as in a bad weather situation?
Do your students know the procedure for different tasks in the classroom?
Have all consequences, where applicable, been communicated to students?

Discussion Point: Briefly share how you have created a community of learners in your classroom with each other. Share how you may improve the classroom management system you currently have. Share what is working in your classroom with each other. Now, spend some time to pray for each other, asking for God's blessings on your classroom management systems.

Closing Prayer: Heavenly Father, thank you for our lesson this week. We want to see an increase in the sense of community in our classroom. Direct us how to ensure all our students feel a part of our classroom learning community. Thank you in advance for all you will do in each of our classes.

Topic: Words

Hear: Psalm 19:14 "Let the words of my mouth and the meditation of my heart be acceptable in Your sight, O Lord, my strength and my redeemer."

Believe: Have you ever been caught in a situation where helping someone back fired? The result being that you become the object of disrespect through ugly acts or words? This is something many educators can relate to in the classroom or at home. This week's topic scripture verse Psalm 19:14 is a great reminder as educators when dealing with children, family, or co-workers. We must be like David who paid close attention to the words of his mouth and the meditation of his heart. David's highest goal was to ensure his words and meditations were acceptable and pleasing to the Lord-His strength and redeemer. When we align ourselves, as David did, ensuring that the words of our mouth and the meditation of our heart are acceptable and pleasing to the Lord, we show patience, gentleness, and kindness. Those who fire back are dealing with more than their miscommunication with us. There is usually a root cause that is unseen, and our words are critical especially while carrying out our calling as a Christian and a teacher. David was a man after God's own heart. He trained his mouth and heart to please God and we can do the same as educators that love the Lord and our calling.

Application: In what area do you need to ensure the words of your mouth and the meditation of your heat is acceptable and pleasing to the Lord?
Is it in your personal life?
Is it in your marriage?
Is it in your classroom?
Is it with that co-worker that just seems to push your buttons?
Is it when dealing with testing issues?
Is it when dealing with students who are not always respectful?
Is it when dealing with students who seem to push you to the limit?

Discussion Point: Briefly share some of the areas you are struggling in with each other. Prayerfully brainstorm better ways to respond to some of the issues in a godly way that will please the Lord.   Now ask God to help you respond to others in a loving and kind way.

Closing Prayer: Lord thank you for the scriptures that confirm these issues are not new nor are the answers to these issues. Help us to respond with words of love, patience and kindness so that our words will be acceptable to you our Lord. Steady our hearts as we look to you for daily strength.

3rd Six Weeks Grading Period: Week 4

Topic: Trust

Hear: Psalm 20:7 "Some trust in chariots, and some in horses; but we will remember the name of the Lord our God."

Believe: In this week's scripture verse, it takes us back to David's time, when chariots were the greatest technology and man's input was their own understanding of how to make them faster, stronger, and safer. Compare those ancient times with the times we live in now - the speed of how we're able to get around on land, water and air. In this week's scripture, David mentions horses; which were known for their natural strength resulting in their trustworthiness. This scripture does an excellent job of reminding us to remember the name of the Lord our God and to trust in Him alone and not man. Not just in education, but in life, it is easy to put our trust in the wrong places at times. We trust in our understanding, or even the education we have, and lately we place our trust in the newest technology. We tend to forget as humans, that we are limited. Only God is unlimited, and He usually must empty us of ourselves, before He can use us. This emptying ensures our total reliance on God. It is only when we remember the name of the Lord our God and trust in Him with all our heart, that He will direct our path and use us for His glory.

Application: In what areas of your life do you need to trust the Lord and stop leaning on your own understanding?
Is it in your personal life?
Is it with your own children?
Is it in your classroom?
Is it with your students?
Is it with your colleagues?
Is it with your church family?

Discussion Point: Briefly share some areas you need to turn over to the Lord with each other. Affirm your trust in God by committing those areas to Him in prayer. Now ask God in prayer to help you lean not on your own understanding but to trust in Him with all your heart.

Closing Prayer: Abba Father, thank you for the knowledge that you have about everything in my life. No one has the knowledge needed to direct my path like You do; thank you for reminding me I can trust You when I call upon your name. I affirm my total dependence on you, my Lord.

3rd Six Weeks Grading Period: Week 5

Topic: Serving

Hear: 1 Timothy 4:16 "Take heed to yourself and to the doctrine. Continue in them, for in doing this you will save both yourself and those who hear you."

Believe: Educators are natural givers by nature. We love to serve others and our days are filled serving our students and their parents. We know our work is vital and the Lord will not forget our work. Yes, it is important that we fulfill the calling the Lord has given us, but we cannot forget our own spiritual needs in the process. We will have nothing to share if our well is dry; with nothing left to give out. This type of state is not good stewardship. In this week's scripture verse, we can gain insight from Paul's instruction to Timothy. Timothy was the senior pastor in the world's largest church in Ephesus. He was living out the great commission of sharing the gospel. His ministry also included dealing with the many issues found in such a large congregation. Paul, his mentor and coach, cautions his brother in Christ to make sure he is paying attention to his own spiritual needs. This is the same admonition for us as educators; we must take care of our relationship with the Lord by spending time with Him. When we spend time with the Lord, our spirit is renewed, and our cup runs over. In this state, we have something to give out joyfully. When we neglect our spiritual needs, we are unable to serve others effectively.

Application: When was the last time you put your spiritual needs first?
Do you have a time set aside each day to nourish your spirit?
Do you spend some time each day in worship?
Do you take time to read God's word and meditate on it daily?
Do you spend time with colleagues in prayer each week?
Do you allow others to serve you when possible?

Discussion Point: Briefly share what you sense the Holy Spirit is teaching you from the scripture verse about stewarding your spiritual life well. Also, share some of your answers to the application questions with each other.

Closing Prayer: Thank you Father for quickening us each day to be sensitive to taking care of our relationship with you. Help us to be diligent disciples by paying close attention to meeting our spiritual needs through Your Word, worship, and fellowship with other disciples. Holy Spirit fill us in areas where we are currently depleted. Energize us by the power of our inner man so we will be strong, sharpened and prepared to serve joyfully on our campuses.

3rd Six Weeks Grading Period: Week 6

Topic: Love

Hear: Galatians 5:22 "But the fruit of the Spirit is love, joy, peace, forbearance, kindness, goodness, faithfulness."

Believe: Students in our public schools come from different walks of life, economic status and various backgrounds. Despite this, there is one thing they all have in common - their need to be loved. God demonstrated His great love for us through His action. He sent His only Son to the cross for our redemption. It was love that sent Jesus Christ to the cross to be bruised for our iniquities. And by His stipes we have been healed. In our scripture verse, we see a different kind of love - *agape love*. Agape love is the highest form of love that is sacrificial in nature. It is a supreme love that knows no limit, not even in dimensions: width, height, or depth. This love transcends time and space. We can only have, and function in, agape love through the power of the Holy Spirit. This love is ours and as Christians we are to share this sacrificial love with our students, families, co-workers, etc. Therefore, we need a consistent relationship with God to refuel our agape love tank. Only through agape love will we be able to fulfill our callings as educators and grow in the fruit of the spirit of love. What we will see flowing out of our lives is an action backed life of love to each student in our classrooms.

Application: Is there any area in your life where you are challenged to know God's love or to share God's love?
In what ways can you share God's love with your students this week?
In what ways can you share God's love with your administrators this week?
In what ways can you share God's love with your co-workers this week?

Discussion Point: Reflect on some of the areas where you are struggling to know God's agape love for you. Also, assess yourself in how you share the agape love the Lord has freely given you through the fruit of the spirit with others. Discuss your reflection and assessment with each other. Now, ask God for His help to address any area you currently feel challenged in receiving and/or sharing agape love.

Closing Prayer: Abba Father, we come to you today asking for your help in receiving and sharing your gift of agape love. Lord, we realize this is a sacrificial love and we need your grace to live this out with all our students. Fill us to overflowing with your agape love, so we can share it freely with those that need it and those that do not know your love for them yet. May they learn of your agape love through the love that we share with them. Thank you, Lord, for Your love! Amen.

Topic: Focus

Hear: Isaiah 26:3 "You will keep him in perfect peace whose mind is stayed on you because he trusts in you."

Believe: There are many circumstances and situations that can take away one's attention from helping students learn. Overcrowded classrooms, non-compliance of parents or students and behavioral issues can really affect the instructional environment. Amid it all, the focus should remain on helping students succeed. This task sometimes can be insurmountable without the help of God. He is our peace during a storm. He will help us regain our focus on what really matters. When we believe, acknowledge, trust and rely on God, He will bathe us in His perfect peace that surpasses all understanding. This is what will help us endure those hard times of teaching.

Application: What are some things you can do differently to help you stay focused?

What are those things that easily distracts you?

List at least 2 known distractors that's difficult for you to recover from and why?

Write down your answers in your journal and use it as a reflective piece when you feel distracted. Trust God for peace in your heart to help you overcome so He can be glorified. Remember, God is the same yesterday, today and forever and when you win, He's pleased. You'll never know who's watching how you respond to your distractions. Your response(s) can possibly be someone else's cure to doubt and unbelief.

Discussion Point: Briefly share with each other what does experiencing God's peace means to you.

Closing Prayer: Heavenly Father, thank you for being our Jehovah Shalom, "God of Peace." You're a loving God that wants your children to experience your fruit of peace in their lives every day. Your word promises that you will keep us in perfect peace if our minds stay focused on you. Help us God to stay focused on you in difficult circumstances and situations. Help us not to overreact and stay focused because with your help all things are possible. In Jesus' name, Amen!

Topic: Diligence

Hear: Proverbs 8:17 "I love those who love me, and those who seek me diligently will find me."

Believe: Being an educator requires hard work and patience to be successful and truly make a significant difference in students' lives. The everyday struggles of trying to teach in the chaos of systems not being in place, behavior issues, etc., really challenges every fiber of an educator's being. But, without the implementation of hard work and patience, students will not benefit if every effort is not pursued. Students don't care about how much a teacher knows, but they do need to know that you care for them. Also, that you are committed to helping them learn and grow. Trusting God enough to believe that He will reward our efforts and will help our patience mature is the foremost important element in overcoming students' weaknesses. Hence, it is important to demonstrate your love for God by diligently seeking Him as your signature for success.

Application: Do you diligently prepare for class every day or is this an area of weakness? Explain.

What does giving your all to your students mean to you?

What is your definition of diligence?

Is there someone who demonstrates diligence that you would like to emulate and why?

Record your responses in your journal for further reflection. When you seek God diligently, life becomes simplified because He will change your perspective and show you how to work smarter and not harder. He will also give you the patience necessary to not become weary while working harder even when things appear not to be changing quickly.

Discussion Point: Briefly share a time with one another that you really worked hard on something and felt like giving up but did not. Share to encourage each other what kept you from giving up?

Closing Prayer: Father God, your word says that patience has to have her perfect work and that there is profit in all labor. Father God, we need your help to be strengthened so we are not weary in well doing. Remind us of our callings when we feel like giving up and that our students' success depends on our diligence and hard work as educators. We ask and thank you for helping us stay the course. In Jesus' name, Amen!

Topic: Action

Hear: I John 4:8 "He who does not love, does not know God, for God is love."

Believe: During the beginning of the school year, it's so easy to love all your students and colleagues as well because you're still learning them and they're still learning you. You're patient and kind to everyone. No one gets on your nerves and all your students are polite and kind to you and to one another. Fast forward to the current grading period; now you may have students that normally do well that are beginning to talk back and be disrespectful. Now these students are interrupting classroom instructions. You have conferences with parents and students but nothing seems to work at this point. Do you stoop to the level of your students and become disrespectful too? Or do you choose to act on God's word and believe what He says, "He who does not love, does not know God." Faith is believing and acting on the word of God which means not acting reactional and emotional. So, you choose to love your students.

Application: Do you react (saying and doing whatever comes to mind)?
Do you respond (apply the word of God to the situation) to chaotic situations in your classroom?
How can you demonstrate the love of God to disrespectful students?
Do you believe it's necessary to forgive to walk in love with others? If so, why?

Acting on God's word helps us to live out God honoring ways. Trust and believe that God is for you and not against you. He will show you how to love the unlovable. God wants His children to be able to do good in the presence of evil and to put His word into action, so He can get involved and turn things around for the glory of His name.

Discussion Point: Briefly share with each other a situation where you demonstrated the love of God even when it was difficult for you to. You chose to act in love instead. Encourage each other as you share those situations that challenged your love walk but you overcame by acting in love.

Closing Prayer: Heavenly Father, you are a God of love. You can never fail us because love never fails. Thank you for loving us while we were still sinners. Thank you for your continuous forgiveness of our sins. Father God you sent your Son to die on the cross for each of us to demonstrate your love for us. You saw past our failures and loved us anyway. Help us to love like you do. Help us to love our students beyond their failures. Help us to live and act out love unconditionally. In Jesus' name, Amen!

Topic: Armor of God

Hear: Ephesians 6:10-11 "Finally, my brethren, be strong in the Lord and in the power of His might, put on the whole armor of God, that you might be able to stand against the wiles of the devil."

Believe: Professional attire is very important in our field of work. We are expected to adhere to a high standard of dressing. The way we dress oftentimes reflects how we feel about ourselves and the job. As Christians, we have a higher call for attire; which is our spiritual attire known as "The Armor of God." This is because as believers we are in a spiritual warfare and we must maintain our "battle-stance," not against co-workers, parents or students, but against satanic, unseen forces. The struggles of teaching with all the demonic forces attempting to influence us negatively are real and we must be prepared. Our defense is in putting on the whole armor of God as stated in our scripture verse. Our armor includes: Belt of Truth, Breastplate of Righteousness, Shod feet with preparation of the gospel of peace, Shield of Faith, Helmet of Salvation and the Sword of the Spirit, which is the word of God. To fasten all the pieces of our armor requires prayer that is the glue that holds the armor together. With this armor we are ready to actively engage in battle.

Application: How is your daily prayer life? Is daily prayer necessary in a Christian's life?
What are your thoughts on praying for those who might have done your wrong? Is this Biblical?
Why do you think it is important to out on the armor of God? Explain.
Write your answers in your journal and reflect on how God wants you to handle battles you encounter. We must trust the process God has mandated us to implement in order to become victorious Christians. He knows that the best way to fight darkness is not with darkness but with the word of God (Sword of the Spirit).

Discussion Point: Share with your colleagues how you currently handle struggles, disappointments and setbacks. Now share how putting on the armor of God can help you to be victorious in these situations.

Closing Prayer: Heavenly Father, thank you for reminding us to put on our armor daily. Thank you for showing us how to position our "battle-stance" against Satan's fiery darts and scheming tactics. Help us to walk in truth, righteousness, peace, faith and your word. Thank you for protecting our minds with purity and giving us hope with the Helmet of Salvation by increasing our expectations of victories in all battles. In Jesus' name, Amen!

4th Six Weeks Grading Period: Week 5

Topic: Relationships

Hear: I Corinthians 3:10 "According to the grace of God which was given to me, as a wise master builder I laid the foundation, and another builds on it. But let each one take heed how he builds on it."

Believe: Building positive and meaningful interpersonal relationships should be a priority in every school community. The success of students should always be a major focus when building relationships. As social creatures we strive to belong and develop good friendships and relationships with positive interactions so it's imperative how and why we build them. We should intentionally strive to be our brother's keeper because what affects one affects others. God places high priority on how we treat and relate to one another. He established relationships and laid out a foundation in His word to show the necessary attributes of building caring ones. Research shows that in schools with high student achievement, caring relationships played a major role in the success of students. The same can be said about low student achievement. It takes a village to successfully help students learn and grow. Each student matters and through the building of strong, healthy relationships we can make sure that no student is left behind. Have you ever thought to ask God whom you should build a relationship with? Ask Him because He will never guide you wrong.

Application: What do you look for when establishing collegial relationships?

How important is it to you that everyone approves and like you? Explain.
Do you know of relationships that were formed that weren't for the best interest of students? Record your answers in your journal and further reflect on them as a means of checks and balances for future relationships. God is waiting for us to involve Him in our relationship building. He knows the minds and hearts of every person and knows what is best for us. Give Him a try. He will never fail you.

Discussion Point: Share with each other about a time you formed a relationship with someone and later regretted doing so? Why was this the case? Encourage each other in what to look for in building godly relationships.

Closing Prayer: Heavenly Father, show and help us with building caring and meaningful relationships that helps students succeed and bring glory to you. Father God, we are relying on you to help us stay the course and focus on what really matters - students' success. With you God all things are possible, and we know that the good work that you started in us, you will finish. In Jesus' name, Amen.

4th Six Weeks Grading Period: Week 6

Topic: Encouragement

Hear: Proverbs 12:25 "Anxiety in a man's heart weighs it down, but a good (encouraging) word makes it glad."

Believe: Unexpected happenings, debilitating roadblocks, and demanding duties can drain educators of the joy of influencing those within our sphere. Yet, when we are discouraged by bewildering circumstances, a simple and sincere word of encouragement can lift our focus and give us the courage and confidence to complete the tasks before us. We have a choice; to either live by our anxious feelings or to live beyond them. A timely word of encouragement helps us to live beyond the things that weigh us down, especially this time of year.

Application: Who needs a word of encouragement today in your sphere of influence?

Is that person your student? Your co-worker? Or your family member?

Who feels like a failure today? Encourage that person today.

Who received a heart-wrenching diagnosis? Encourage that person today.

Who heard a conversation that causes one to think that divorce is imminent?

Sometimes, we think that our situation is unbearable. Yet, a quick look around us confirms that everyone is burdened with things that weigh them down. Today, students carry heavier burdens than they should for their age. So, what are we to do? In our fast-paced, day-to-day activities, we should realize that it only takes a moment to speak a power-packed, thoughtful word of encouragement over a student, co-worker, or family member. Yes, it only takes a moment.

Discussion Point: Briefly share with each other about a person in your lives who uplifts your heart through thoughtful spoken words of encouragement. Pray blessings on that person. Now pray and ask God that each of you will become encouragers in your spheres of influence.

Closing Prayer: Heavenly Father, thank you for Your watchful care over us. Thank you for those around us who speak timely words of encouragement to us especially in our times of need. In return, give us Your eyes to see the disheartened who need a power-packed, thoughtful word of encouragement from us today. We ask this in Jesus name. Amen.

5th Six Weeks Grading Period: Week 1

Topic: Praise

Hear: Psalm 150:6 "Let everything that has breath praise the Lord. Praise ye the Lord."

Believe: We are living in a time when giving thanks for everything is not even a concept to most, but it is the will of God, in Christ Jesus, for us to give thanks. Despite difficulties and hard circumstances, we can surely find reasons to thank God. Tammy is a vibrant educator that had breast cancer. Despite her situation, she had many things to thank God for like God never leaving her nor forsaking her, her church, her supporting family, encouraging friends, the peace of God through each surgery and her decision to purchase cancer insurance the year which provided more than enough money to pay for her medical expenses. Her insurance policy paid her so much money that she was able to pay off a debt on her house from a contractor who had taken $42,000 and done nothing but left a hole in her back yard. God saw her and her family through one of the darkest times of her life. Tammy was able to praise God, not for the cancer, but for all the good that came through the breast cancer. Praise exhibits our dependence on God, draws out our trust even in darkness, and shows our obedience for the One who died for us while also revealing that He now lives in us. And, one of the best reasons to praise is that when we praise, we are focused on God and not on ourselves. What we end up with for praising God despite our circumstances is joy; which in turn becomes our strength.

Application: What do you need to praise God for today despite your circumstances?
What are some things that are hindering your praise to God?
Is it your job?
Is it unanswered prayers?
Did someone get the position you wanted?
Is it in dealing with the most difficult student you have ever had?
Is it a challenging relationship with a co-worker?

Discussion Point: Take some time to discuss with your colleagues and reflect on a situation or situations that have robbed you of praising the Lord and receiving all the benefits of your praise. Follow up the discussion by praying for each other to experience God's strength and grace.

Closing Prayer: Lord help us to be thankful in all things as we trust You. Help us to trust You that you have the perfect plan for us. Create a hunger of praise in us for who You are. Lord may we praise You all the days of our lives. Lord, may we praise You and not the rocks on our behalf. Let everything that has breath praise the Lord! We praise You today, Lord!

5th Six Weeks Grading Period: Week 2

Topic: Proximity

Hear: James 4:8 "Draw close to God, and He will draw close to you."

Believe: In topology math, proximity is defined as the nearness of space. This week's scripture verse gives us an assurance - that if we draw close to God, He, in turn, will draw close to us. What a wonderful promise we have been given! Even though we have this great promise, the distractions of the world have left many of us distanced from God. Therefore, it is so important to schedule and guard our time with God, so the enemy does not snatch it away from us. One way to draw close to God, is through this weekly Bible Study where we get the opportunity to allow the Word of God to dwell richly in us. In so doing, the Word of God will be part of our lives, because when we do, the Word of God will enrich with spiritual wisdom and insight making us rich beyond measure. And when we are rich in our spirits, we will have an overflow of worship and counsel to freely share with those in need; especially our students who are struggling. God wants to draw close to us; but we must take the first step out of our love and desire to be with God. It is like any friendship; we want friends that want to be our friend and not a forced relationship. By drawing close to God, we are saying to Him, we want to be His friend. This divine friendship with God is spiritual wealth. Just imagine the abundant blessing of the God of the universe wanting to draw close to us.

Application: What are some things in your life that are hindering you from drawing close to God?
What are some distractions in your way of daily reading the Word of God?
Is your schedule so over booked that you do not have time to spend with God?
Do you need help in how to spend time with God?
Are you so helping others at home, school, and church that you neglect your own spiritual life?
Does your family know how important your time with God is?

Discussion Point: Take some time to discuss, share and encourage each other on practical ways to draw close to God. Share your thoughts about reading and keeping a spiritual journal to record your spiritual journey. Also share your thoughts with each other about setting spiritual goals and writing down answers to prayers as they come.

Closing Prayer: Abba Father, help and quicken us about creating a schedule for drawing close to You. Strengthen and guide us to protect our time with You. Lord we believe when we draw close to You that You will draw close to us. Create a new hunger in us to look forward to our time together. We want to be spiritually rich in wisdom, so that we may be a vessel of Your love, mercy, grace, and truth to others; especially our students and parents. In Jesus name, Amen.

Topic: Fear

Hear: Isaiah 43:1 "But now, this is what the Lord says - He who created you, Jacob, He who formed you, Israel: "Do not fear, for I have redeemed you; I have summoned you by name; you are mine.""

Believe: Camille loves teaching and just finished her first year of teaching. As part of her summer, she had the opportunity to learn about creativity in gifted and talented (GT) students while attending a professional development conference. During the session, the presenter noted that most GT students are extremely gifted in creativity and thinking in ways that are extraordinary. However, they have experienced multiple rejections from peers or teachers in the past, which caused them to limit their own creative abilities in order to appear "normal". At this point, the Lord spoke to Camille about how she relates to GT students, even though she does not consider herself GT. She realized that fear of failure and rejection had prevented her from doing many things in life. In this week's scripture verse, the Lord is reminding us as educators, that we have nothing to fear. He also reminds us that we are not stuck in our mistakes, or in our future missteps. He does so by reminding us that He has redeemed us implying that He already has covered our failures past, present, and future. With this powerful perspective, launch out and take off the limits on yourself.

Application: Do you fear failure or making mistakes?
Do you see God as the Lord of your life; trusting that He already has gone ahead of you and has you covered?
How is God using the mistakes in your past to help your future?
How can you use a lesson from your mistakes to help your students?
Have you extended grace to students when they have made mistakes?

Discussion Point: Briefly share some situations where you have feared messing up and how the Lord worked it for your good. Encourage each other this week with Romans 8:28. Read it together.

Closing Prayer: Father, thank you for redeeming us from our failures. Thank you for giving us peace and for working out every mistake that we make for our good. Help us to look to you to be our strength and guide this week, in Jesus' name Amen.

Topic: Answer

Hear: Psalm 119: 105 "Thy word is a lamp unto my feet, and a light unto my path."

Believe: It was 4:45 AM, and Kaley had just dialed the 17-digit international telephone number and got an unfamiliar ringing tone. She tried again and again but still got the same unfamiliar tone. She knew the tone well, since her extended family lives in Chile and she typically makes international calls at least once a week. Suddenly it occurred to Kaley to re-check the number her older sister had texted her the night before. She checked the text message and to her utter surprise, it was a 16-digit number. Kaley had accidentally added another number that made the phone number 17 digits. That explained the unfamiliar ring tone she got when she dialed the number. She tried calling again, this time with the 16-digit number and the call went through. It was right at that point that the Lord began to minister to her heart about how many times we flow through life finding out things are not working as they should. However, we never stop to ask God for answers either through prayer or His word. Many times, we assume that because we have been a Christian for a while, we have all the answers. However, God will normally lead us to His word to find a scripture or story that will have the answers we are seeking. We just have to be humble enough like Kaley to re-check ourselves. God's word is a lamp to our feet and a light to our path. God has the answer; all we must do is ask.

Application: In what area of your life do you need some God answers?
Is it with a student that has been difficult to connect with?
Is it with a co-worker that you seem not to understand each other?
Is it with a parent who is proving challenging?

Discussion Point: Briefly share with each other some of the areas you are needing answers in your teaching practice. Now spend some time to pray for each other asking God for answers. Listen as the Holy Spirit speaks to you.

Closing Prayer: Thank you, Lord for leading and guiding us in your word. We ask that you light our path and understandings in those areas we are needing answers. Illuminate our hearts with your truth and give us the courage we need to follow through. In Jesus name, we pray.

5th Six Weeks Grading Period: Week 5

Topic: Prayer

Hear: Genesis 20:17 "Then Abraham prayed to God, and God healed Abimelech, his wife, and his female servants, so they could have children."

Believe: The evidence that God answers prayer is all over the Bible in both the Old and New Testaments. The Bible hailed Abraham as a man of prayer. The essence of answered prayer is dialogue that is specific and fixed on faith in God. In our scripture verse, Abraham prayed for Abimelech and his family. God heard Abraham's prayer and healed Abimelech, his wife and maidservants so they were able to bear children. Abraham shows us what it takes to have our prayers answered by God - we must believe in God's character and ability to answer prayer. This belief in the character of God is critical to activating our faith when we come to God in prayer. The story of Hannah in 1 Samuel 1:10 is more evidence that God answers prayer. Hannah believed in the character of God and consistently poured her heart out to God in prayer. Hannah prayed with zealous faith and she received the answer to her prayer when God blessed her with a son that she dedicated to the Lord. As Christ's ambassadors in our public schools, educators can bring heaven to earth on campuses through faith-filled prayers for students and parents. The results will be noticeable as heaven permeates the hearts and minds of everyone receiving prayer. Prayer helps ensure our dependence on a faithful God. Prayer is our solid leaning wall that will never let us fall.

Application: Is there anything that inhibits your trust in God?
What do you believe about the character of God?
What prayer needs do you have for your students?
What prayer needs do you have for your family?
What prayer needs do you have for your friends?

Discussion Point: Reflect on the character of God in your life. Share this character of God with each other. This is your building block as you trust God to answer your prayer. Share prayer requests and spend some time to pray over each other's requests.

Closing Prayer: Heavenly Father, help us develop a praying heart and spirit. Teach us to pray your heart for our students, parents and community. Empower us by your Spirit to trust you for answers to our prayers. Thank you for hearing us. We thank you in advance for answers, in Jesus name.

5th Six Weeks Grading Period: Week 6

Topic: Integrity

Hear: Proverbs 11:3 "The integrity of the upright guides them, but the unfaithful are destroyed by
their duplicity."

Believe: Public school educators are faced with many decisions throughout the school year. Schedules and the workload can be very challenging at times and difficult to keep up with. Administrators are not always watching or monitoring every step that teachers make. This is where personal integrity comes in for Christians: see yourself living out Proverbs 11:3 daily in your school. Do what is right, because it is the right thing to do and not what is easy. Integrity is everything. Integrity is doing the right thing when no one is watching. However, our heavenly Father is watching and never misses anything. He is keeping a record for that day when each Christian that has accepted His salvation and Lordship will see Him face-to-face. Doing the right thing no matter what is a form of worship to God. He longs for His children to worship Him with truth and honesty.

Application: What are some situations during this school year that challenged your honesty or integrity?
With family members? With students? With parents? With colleagues? With campus leaders? With assessment data? With daily requirements? With your special students?
To help prepare you to do the right thing no matter what, visualize these situation outcomes and how you would respond if you were honest and when you were not honest. Now record in your journal and describe how you felt knowing you did the right thing while no one was watching. The reality and truth are that, God was watching everything, and He knows our hearts. Educating students is one of the most challenging professions. However, Christians are not left helpless. God is with us every step of the way. The encouragement is that sometimes integrity means enduring short-term pain for longer term gains. Integrity is developed over time.

Discussion Point: Briefly share some of the challenging decisions you may be facing with your colleagues. See if anyone has some insight or potential solutions. Now take those challenging decisions to God in prayer together.

Closing Prayer: Heavenly Father, thank you for your love, grace, and mercies which are new every morning. We commit every decision we make to you. We are trusting you to help us increase our level of integrity and build our character. Our desire as your children is to glorify Your name.

Topic: Peace

Hear: Hebrews 12:14 "Make every effort to live in peace with everyone and to be holy; without holiness no one will see the Lord."

Believe: It is the last grading period of the school year and things get tougher with end-of-year assessments, requirements and activities. As we move farther into the school year, we are bound to face different trials, unexpected changes, relationship struggles, and struggling students. Then we have special challenges with parents and sometimes new district mandates. Things seem to go chaotic this time of year. However, as Christ's ambassadors we are peace carriers and called to be peacemakers. No matter how chaotic a situation or place may be, we have the Holy Spirit and His fruit of peace growing and expressing God's heart through us. As God's hands and feet, we must live in peace with everyone as stated in our scripture verse, despite any trials we may be facing. As peace carriers and peacemakers, we can trust and believe that God has our back. And because of this truth, we have nothing to worry or be burdened about. We can allow the peace of God to rule.

Application: What sort of trials are you currently facing?

Do you have a new administrator?

Have you just been assigned a new leadership role with extra responsibilities?

Do you have any colleague that is a first-year teacher?

Are there any new adjustments with your own family?

As you reflect on these questions, begin speaking peace into each situation. God is the only one that can give perfect peace. Trust God to handle these situations and see you through the end of the school year. Supernatural is a gift we can live in as children of God. Let God's peace rule your heart.

Discussion Point: Briefly share with each other some of the trials or struggles you might be facing this last grading period of the school year. Spend some time to pray for each other for God's peace.

Closing Prayer: Heavenly Father, thank you for taking all our struggles and trials as we are lay them down at your feet. We cast all our cares upon you, because we know you care for us. We release all our burdens to you and ask for your supernatural peace to rule and reign in our hearts, mind and souls. We lean on your faithfulness to take care of us. Thank you, for having our backs.

6th Six Weeks Grading Period: Week 2

Topic: Endurance

Hear: Galatians 6:9 "Let not us become weary in doing good, for at the proper time we will reap a harvest if we do not give up."

Believe: As educators, we might be faced with providing support to challenging students and parents, a new team of teachers, or even the daily tasks of trying to balance work and home life. You might be thinking this is a bit much and when will it end. The feelings are valid and sometimes it looks like the finish line is so far away, especially this last grading period. However, this is not the time to quit. This is the time to activate endurance and keep going. This is when educators must have faith and continue to run the race set before us. Our scripture verse for this week shines the light on endurance. The scripture further admonishes us why we should not give up; because at the proper time we reap the harvest if we do not give up. The reward is not in the middle, it is at the end, which means we must finish and not give up. As a Christian, there is strength available to continue the race till the end of the school year, despite all the obstacles we might encounter.

Application: What is making endurance difficult for you?

Who or what is making you want to give up?

Why do you think endurance in important in our profession as well as our daily lives?

Think of an athlete and what he/she must endure in a race. As you reflect and ponder the answers to the application questions, remind yourself of your "why" and commitment to your calling and family. Remind yourself of your Savior - Jesus Christ the Son of God who endured and carried the Cross for us. During His journey He encountered many distractions and struggles. The load of the cross was heavy, but He never gave up. Jesus is our perfect example of endurance. He understands and will see you to the finish line this school year.

Discussion Point: Briefly share with each other about any hindrance you might need to get rid of, in other to run better. Now, spend some time to pray over each other for strength for the journey.

Closing Prayer: Heavenly Father, we thank you that you are a big God and there is nothing too difficult or hard for you. You see and know the long race that is before us and we ask that you help us to run with endurance. When we feel like giving up, we will remember that you have us in your hands and will help us to finish this school year strong in Jesus Name.

Topic: Patience

Hear: Colossians 3:12 "Therefore, as God's chosen people, holy and dearly loved, clothe yourselves with compassion, kindness, humility, gentleness and patience."

Believe: Our profession has many irritants that can cause daily frustration if allowed. From preparing for different events throughout the school year, results from student assessments, reluctant students, or waiting for a response from parents, the opportunities for frustration are plenty. It's in those frustrating times, that we must put to remembrance our scripture verse that admonishes us to action. These pieces of attire are just what we need to overcome the many irritants during this time of year. We need the attire of compassion, kindness, humility, gentleness and patience to combat the frustrations that come with this time of year. The best part of our scripture verse; is the fact that we are God's chosen people. That means, we are not by ourselves. As a farmer must be patient for his harvest, so we must exercise patience in dealing with end-of-school year frustrations. And we are not meant to do this alone because we have an anchor.

Application: Do you have students in your class who seem to test your patience?

What advice would you give a colleague who might be struggling with patience?

Can you see how patience is a virtue?

Do you respond to stressful situation without getting upset?

As you reflect on these questions, meditate on the scripture verse. Write down your answers in your journal. Remember that patience is waiting for something or someone without getting upset. Always think about having a positive outcome and good attitude in your time of waiting.

Discussion Point: Briefly share with each other how developing patience can make you healthier emotionally. Discuss anything during this grading period that frustrates you or tests your patience.

Closing Prayer: Heavenly Father, thank you for your loving kindness and long suffering towards us. Thank you, Holy Spirit for developing patience in us and activating our self-control when we are faced with stressful situations. We ask that You empower our inner man. We trust you to help us finish strong. We commit the remainder of the school year to you, in Jesus name.

6th Six Weeks Grading Period: Week 4

Topic: Courage

Hear: Joshua 1:9 "Have I not commanded you? Be strong and courageous. Do not be afraid; do not be discouraged, for the Lord your God will be with you wherever you go."

Believe: In 2010, the world watched as 33 Chilean miners were rescued. These courageous men found a way to stay alive trapped hundreds of feet below the surface for 17 days before they were found. Then it took another four months after they were found before they were finally rescued. We saw firsthand the triumph of the human spirit. These men lived in great uncertainty and determined to stay alive. In a similar manner, working in education involves many uncertainties and heartaches. Educators tend to feel these unpleasantries are caused by decisions made by district or campus administrators. Take for example a position change or loss of an assistant or paraprofessional. What we must understand, as Christians, is that these decisions are not personal but simply necessary. In this week's scripture verse, God commands us to be strong and courageous which means we must determine we will finish well and not bow down to fear.

Application: What are some situations you have faced this school year that caused you to be afraid or live in fear?

How do you exhibit courage daily?

What can block courage from operating in and through your life?

Who is the source of your courage in times of uncertainty?

When faced with uncertainty, the best thing to do is wait on the Lord. This seems easy, yet it is hard sometimes to wait on God. Instead of choosing fear in the face of uncertainty, choose to trust God completely. As educators we need courage to make tough decisions in our classrooms.

Discussion Point: Share with each other a time during the school year when you were faced with difficulty or intimidation. Also, discuss some of the uncertainty you might be facing as the school year ends. Celebrate all the great things each of you have done this school year. Thank God for them.

Closing Prayer: Heavenly Father, thank you that you are the God of love and peace. We trust you with everything. Thank you for the confidence of your word this week. Help us to finish this year strong and well. We turn all concerns and important decisions about the remaining school year to you. We thank you in advance, in Jesus name.

6th Six Weeks Grading Period: Week 5

Topic: Friendship

Hear: 1 Samuel 23: 18 "The two of them made a covenant before the Lord. Then Jonathan went home, but David remained at Horesh."

Believe: The old adage of "A friend in need is a friend indeed" is a true saying. God created humans with a desire to experience true friendship. As Christians, we desire true and godly friends that can be trusted. Good friends love at all times. Many of us have high school friendships that, though we do not get to see each other often, that strong bond of friendship has lasted throughout the years. Reunions tend to validate these long-term friendships with rambunctious celebrations and excitement of seeing each other again. Our scripture verse sheds light to this type of true, loyal and godly friendship. David was running for his life due to King Saul's plan to kill him. Yet we see a strong friendship formed between Saul's son Jonathan and David. Jonathan traveled to Horesh to meet with David where he encouraged, helped David to find strength in the Lord and assured his safety. He made a covenant with David sealing their friendship. As educators we need each other and we need covenant friendships to stand strong amid our hectic schedules, workloads, demands and callings.

Application: What are some characteristics of a good friend?

Were you able to develop some new friendships this school year?

Jonathan exemplified covenant friendship with David. He was not thinking of himself though he was heir to the throne. He placed David's interest above his and wanted the best for him. This is the mark of true friendship. As Christian educators we need covenant friendships to grow and stay accountable in our calling. Covenant friendships guide us in imitating the legacy of Jesus Christ our Savior and Lord who loves unconditionally. Reflect on these types of friendships in your life.

Discussion Point: Share with each other what some of your characteristics are for a good friend. Discuss ways your friendships have been strengthened this school year. Discuss ways to cultivate covenant friendships with each other. Discuss ways to keep each other accountable even when school is out for the summer break. Share one encouraging word with each other and pray for each other.

Closing Prayer: Dear Lord, thank you for showing us through the life of Your Son, what unconditional love looks like. Because of His love for us, Jesus Christ went to the cross enduring pain, shame and suffering. Help us to be such good friends to each other. In Jesus name we pray. For

Topic: Warrior

Hear: Judges 6:12 "When the angel of the Lord appeared to Gideon, he said, "The Lord is with you, mighty warrior.""

Believe: At every stage of life, we see battles. As Christians we are in a spiritual battle that never ends. However, we do not battle against flesh and blood; rather our fight is against the spiritual powers of this world. Each world system is pitted against the purpose and will of God. It takes Christians who know who they are in Christ to combat these spiritual powers of the world. From our daily instruction to the growth of all our students, there is a spiritual battle to ensure we as Christian educators do not attain our goals and callings. Therefore, we must adopt the mindset of a warrior that is always prepared for battle. Since, the challenges that comes with each school day is different, we need to be ready to combat the challenges as they come. Our scripture verse reminds us that as Gideon, we are warriors in the battle of education. We are warriors in the battle for our students minds and lives. We are warriors in the battle for our schools, campuses and communities. As the Lord was with Gideon, so He is with every child of His that has committed his or her life to Jesus Christ. We do not fight alone. God is with us; this is what makes us strong, confident, courageous and bold in the face of unsurmountable challenges in our classrooms. As we close out the school year, celebrate the fact that you made it warrior educator! God celebrates you that you stood well all through the year; despite all the hardships, trials, hurts, demands and assessments. The Lord commends you, warrior educator!

Application: What are some major personal milestones to celebrate?

What are some major milestones to celebrate for your students?

What are some major milestones to celebrate for your family?

What are some major milestones to celebrate for your colleagues?

What are some major milestones to celebrate for your campus?

Discussion Point: Share with each other all the major milestones you have had individually and collectively. Discuss what made each of those celebrations as memorable. Now thank God together for keeping you through the school year! Also, spend some time in prayer for your students, parents and administrators.

Closing Prayer: Heavenly Father, we offer our gratitude and thanks for a completed school year. Thank you for helping us through each grading cycle. We give you all the praise and glory for this year!

Educator's Compass: Schools on 9 Weeks Grading Period Schedule

Topic: Speak it into Existence

Hear: Genesis 1:1 "In the beginning God created the heavens and the earth."

Believe: A new school year brings with it new adventures and excitement. Imagine, you were part of the team when Genesis 1:1 happened. From absolutely nothing, God speaks, and then things begin to appear in heaven and on earth. As a Christian, you have that same power of the Holy Spirit to **speak things into existence**. This is called "faith."

Application: What are some things you would like to see happen this school year?

For you?

For your family?

For your students?

For your colleagues?

For your campus?

For your district?

For your community?

Write them down in your journal. Now take each of those things you have written down and "speak" them into existence in prayer. Take each of the things written down to God in prayer. You can speak into existence this new school year. Though, you don't know everything that will happen this school year, God does, and you can commit this new school year into His care. Close out your prayer time with thanksgiving. As God begins to answer each of your requests, be sure to share the testimony with your compass group. It is always an encouragement to others when we share answers to prayers.

Discussion Point: Briefly share with each other how faith is related to prayer.

Closing Prayer: Heavenly Father, thank you for this new school year. I commit my life, my calling and my desires for this school year into your hands. I trust you to make all things work together for my good and for my students, campus and district.

Topic: Increase

Hear: Job 8:7 "Though your beginning was insignificant, yet your end will increase greatly."

Believe: As educators, we sometimes feel inadequate with all the demands of a new school year. With new district and state mandates to implement, new programs, and new students that we are eager to get to know, a new school year might make us feel inadequate and sometimes insignificant. In this Job 8:7 scripture, Bildad (one of Job's friends) though not at first encouraging, gave an inspiring advise that gave Job hope that all be well. As a Christian, there is hope that you will have **increase** this school year, despite what might seem like insurmountable obstacles.

Application: What are some new mandates you are faced with this school year?

What are some new instructional programs you are required to implement this year?

Do you have new students in your class this year?

What are some challenges in your own family this school year?

Do you feel inadequate?

These are all valid feelings for an educator at the beginning of a new school year. As you answer these questions in your journal, receive encouragement from this week's scripture. Despite all these challenges, take courage in knowing that God is with you. God is for you. God is in you. God did not bring you this far, to abandon you. Your end will increase not just a little bit, but greatly. Again, you can have faith in God's faithfulness. As you pray, ask God to increase you greatly. Ask Him to help you meet and exceed all the challenges ahead this school year. Ask God to guide you and empower you to do your part and to do it well for His glory.

Discussion Point: Briefly share some of this new school year's challenges with your compass colleagues and take those to God in prayer together.

Closing Prayer: Heavenly Father, thank you for your faithfulness that You keep covenant and steadfast love with those who love You and keep Your commandments. We turn all these challenges and cares of this new school year into Your powerful hand and trust Your care for us.

1st Nine Weeks Grading Period: Week 3

Topic: Confidence

Hear: Philippians 1:6 "For I am confident of this very thing, that He who began a good work in you will perfect it until the day of Christ Jesus."

Believe: Our American culture prides itself with consumer confidence; an economic indicator that measures the level of confidence consumers feel about the state of the economy and their personal financial situation. In this week's scripture verse, Apostle Paul assures the Philippians about his confidence in the faithfulness of God. Whatever God starts, He finishes. As Christian educators, we might not have all the details of how the school year will go, however, we can rely confidently on the unwavering faithfulness of God. God began a good work in you and that same God will complete what He started in you. This is where our confidence lies - in God's faithfulness, in God's power and in God's track record.

Application: Where do you need God's assurance and affirmation this week?

Is it in your personal life?

Is it in your family?

Is it in your classroom with some of your students who need extra assistance?

Is it with your some of your parents on how to get them on board with the new initiatives?

Is it with your colleagues?

Is it with your workload that seems to grow with each passing day?

Is it the mounting pressure of scaffolding instruction for your students?

Is it the upcoming school activity you have been assigned to lead?

Discussion Point: Briefly share some of the areas you need God's assurance and affirmation this week with your compass colleagues. Now ask God in prayer for the courage and strength to continue to do a good work this school year.

Closing Prayer: Abba Father, thank you for the assurance your word gives me today, that the good work you have begun in me, you will perfect until the day of Christ Jesus.

Topic: Hand of God

Hear: Nehemiah 2:18 "I told them how the hand of my God had been favorable to me and also about the king's words which he had spoken to me. Then they said, "Let us arise and build." so they put their hands to the good work."

Believe: Nehemiah was cupbearer to the king of Persia in 445 BC. He had received the news that the remnant of Jews in Judah were suffering and that the walls of Jerusalem were broken down. Nehemiah's compassion about the situation, moved him into action. He asked the king for permission to return and rebuild the city. The king granted his request. In this week's scripture, Nehemiah visited Jerusalem to see the ruins he had learned about. Nehemiah then went on to share with the officials guarding the ruins, how he got there. Because of the hand of God, Nehemiah received favor both from God and the king. The hand of God is symbolic of the power of God. Miracles happen because of the hand of God. Miracles are remarkable occurrences that cannot be explained with human intellect. The good news is, as Christians we can ask God for a miracle for whatever impossible circumstances we are facing. Only the hand of God can do the impossible on our behalf.

Application: What impossible situation(s) are you facing this week?

In your personal life?

In your family life?

At your school?

No matter the situation, God can be fully trusted. He is a master at performing miracles.

Discussion Point: If you are at liberty, briefly share one or two of the impossible situations you are facing with your compass colleagues. Encourage each other as you pray together.

Closing Prayer: Heavenly Father, we are grateful for your loving kindness towards us. We are resting on your character that you can be fully trusted with all our impossibilities. Just like Nehemiah, we will live to proclaim the greatness of your hand in our lives.

1st Nine Weeks Grading Period: Week 5

Topic: Community

Hear: Hebrews 3:14 "We have come to share in Christ, if indeed we hold our original conviction firmly to the very end."

Believe: School provides a sense of community. A place of shared interest and mission. Each classroom is a community of learners that share experiences together. Hebrews Chapter 3 begins with a general encouragement to Christians who are in community together. Jesus Christ is our Savior and Lord and following Him together helps strengthen our faith. Our work as educators is not an isolation sport. It requires community 24/7. Yet, our educational system has created an isolation culture that sometimes makes it challenging to have community. This is one reason, why many new teachers struggle their first year of teaching. They feel isolated. They feel as if no one understands what they are facing. This week's scripture enlightens us that as Christians, our **community** is based on our Lord Savior, Jesus Christ. As we settle into the new school year, it is important to make community a priority. This compass Bible Study is meant to help achieve that very goal of building a sense of community and camaraderie on your campus. You are not alone. There are other Christians who understand you and are rooting for you and your students to succeed this school year. Determine not to go at it alone this school year. You have your brothers and sisters in Christ with you.

Application: What are some things that give you a sense of community?

At home? At church?

In your classroom?

On your campus?

Within your district?

Discussion Point: Briefly share these things that give you a sense of community. Pay attention to what your colleagues have shared and take note where you have mutual interests besides school. Determine to build and grow together in these areas of interest this school year.

Closing Prayer: Thank you Jesus, for your sacrifice on the cross to make us a community of believers. Help us to develop and grow our community here on this campus this school year.

1st Nine Weeks Grading Period: Week 6

Topic: Celebration

Hear: Ecclesiastes 3:13 "And also that every man should eat and drink, and enjoy the good of all his labor, it is the gift of God."

Believe: We all love a good time and commemorating special life milestones and accomplishments like birthdays, weddings, or graduations. While none of these are happening this week on your campus; it is still cause for celebration. It is the end of the first six weeks grading period! You and your students have braced through some challenging times. From acclimating your new students to your classroom and campus, to engaging parents as partners for the school year, you survived it all. Since the beginning of the school year, you have planned, written and documented at least thirty lesson plans. By now, your students are familiar with your classroom rules and procedures and your class starting to feel like a family. You have been hard at work, working late and arriving early to school. You have established a strong foundation for the school year. So it is time to celebrate! The scripture this week acknowledges the need for celebration after a time or season of hard work. Our scripture verse states the result of your hard work is a gift of God. Whenever you invest any amount of energy, effort, or passion to do something, and it yields a good result, you should celebrate. We have been conditioned by our American culture, to only see success as the end result. However, success is also recognizing the small steps completed during the process of achieving any goal. So today, celebrate! Celebrate your passion to teach. Celebrate your students and all the progress they have made so far. Celebrate your colleagues. Celebrate life. Celebrate you.

Application: What are some things you need to celebrate this week?

From your personal life?

From your students?

From your campus and district?

Discussion Point: Celebrate each other. Share your highs from your life, family, students, community etc. Fill your passion and motivation tank with these celebrations.

Closing Prayer: We are a grateful people. Thank you, Lord for how far you have brought us and helped us. We acknowledge that You are the wind beneath our wings. You are the One that has called us to teach. As we continue our year, empower us to be all we need to be, for your glory.

1st Nine Weeks Grading Period: Week 7

Topic: Light

Hear: Matthew 5:14 "You are the light of the world. A town built on a hill cannot be hidden."

Believe: Light is powerful. Imagine staying at a hotel that uses energy saving technology to turn lights on and off. By simply inserting and removing the room key, you can control the amount of light in the room. Unlike sound waves that are carried by vibrations through a medium, light does not require a medium for it to travel. The speed that light travels is an indication of the effect of light that ambassadors of Jesus Christ carry with them. Light is a form of energy. Light makes things visible. Light alters an atmosphere. Light guides. Light always has a source. The most important takeaway is that without a source, light will be incapable of its various effects. For ambassadors of Jesus Christ, we must also be plugged into the source of life to stay charged up to disseminate darkness. With one grading period under your belt, you can see different ways that your light is shining in your students' lives. The scripture this week, makes a bold declaration on how we must live as Christ's ambassadors. We are "lights" and we must be effective. We must shine. The world is counting on our light to help guide them into purpose. You are a light and must continue to shine!

Application: What are some ways that your light is shining?

In your personal life?

In your family?

At your school?

In your classroom?

Discussion Point: Briefly share with each other how your lights are shining for the Lord. Give God praise for all the ways He is working in each of your compass colleagues. Let your lights shine for Jesus Christ our Lord and Savior.

Closing Prayer: Heavenly Father, thank you for sending your son Jesus Christ to pay the ultimate sacrifice for our salvation. This sacrifice is what qualifies us as your light bearers. Help our lights to shine day by day for your glory in all we do and say.

1st Nine Weeks Grading Period: Week 8

Topic: Refuge

Hear: Psalm 46:1 "God is our refuge and strength, an ever-present help in trouble."

Believe: The medieval times are well-known for their fortified moats. These ancient buildings provided shelter and defense for people who were under attack or threatened by war or danger. The buildings were castle-like in nature, with huge doors and high walls. Though many of these buildings were built hundreds of years ago, some can still be found all over Europe and the Middle East. This week's scripture paints a picture for us. Our God the Creator of the heavens and the earth is a refuge. He is strong and can never be defeated in any battle or war. Whatever the attack; be it spiritual or physical we can count on our God's protection and defense. Additionally, we can count on His everlasting strength to carry us through times of difficulty. The best part of God's safety is that He is always available. He is never asleep or on vacation. He is an ever-present help in trouble. He is the best person to call upon when in trouble or distress. As the school year unfolds, many unforeseen challenges are unfolding with it. At this point, we are asking ourselves and each other, "Is it Thanksgiving or Christmas break yet?" It is during times like this that we need to rely on the help of our God. He is our fortified shelter. We can call upon the Lord for strength. We are not defenseless. We have a shelter. We have hope. We have an anchor.

Application: What are you facing today that needs the ever-present help of God?

In your personal life?

In your family?

At your school?

In your classroom?

Discussion Point: If you are at liberty, briefly share one area that you need the ever-present help of God with your compass colleagues. Now take those needs before God in prayer. He is Present.

Closing Prayer: Thank you Lord, that You are a solid refuge, a trusted shelter, a bulwark of strength, and Omnipresent. We cast all our needs on you and ask for your help in our situations.

1st Nine Weeks Grading Period: Week 9

Topic: Strength

Hear: Ephesians 6:10 "Finally, be strong in the Lord and in His mighty power."

Believe: Popeye the Sailor was an all-time favorite family cartoon in the 1960s. Through the years, Popeye has also appeared in comic books and arcade and video games. This fictional character was created by Elzie C. Segar. Popeye was known for his extraordinary strength which he got from eating spinach. His strength allowed him to accomplish incredible physical feats, often defeating the antagonist in the story. Popeye was always seen using his extraordinary strength to rescue others in distress. Ephesians Chapter 6 opens with admonition to different groups of people; children, fathers, servants and masters. After these greetings, the Apostle Paul gives a command. He starts with the word "finally" to communicate the last thought in his series of related admonitions. Paul commands that as followers of Jesus Christ, we must be strong; however not in our strength or our roles. We must be strong in the Lord only and in His mighty power. The Lord's power is enormous. The Lord's power is unparalleled. The Lord's power is transformational. The Lord's power is restorative. The Lord's power is healing. This is the kind of power we are encouraged to be strong in. As the instructional pressure mounts, and the classroom discipline problems arise, you can find strength in the Lord, your Savior, Father, Master, Friend, Counselor, and Advocate. Yes, you can find strength in the Lord, He never runs out of it.

Application: Who or what seems to sap your strength lately?

Is it a specific student?

Is it a demanding parent?

Is it a new assignment?

Is it the new district mandate?

Discussion Point: There is no shame in sharing our areas of need or weakness. Discuss with each other how this week's lesson is applicable to you. As a follow-up, journal your reflections.

Closing Prayer: Dear Lord, we come boldly to the throne of grace to ask for strength in this time of our weakness. Lord, we ask that you sense your nearness in a new way. May Your strength be perfected in us as we trust you with these areas that sap our strength. We thank you in advance.

2nd Nine Weeks Grading Period: Week 1

Topic: Courage

Hear: Joshua 1:9 "Have I not commanded you? Be strong and courageous. Do not be afraid; do not be discouraged, for the Lord your God will be with you wherever you go."

Believe: One of America's sports icons is Jackie Robinson - a man of courage in a time that tested the culture of a society. Jackie Robinson was the first African-American to play baseball in the Major Leagues. Jackie demonstrated great courage during a time in American society when it was unacceptable for African-Americans to play professional baseball. In 1946, Jackie broke that racial barrier. He stood firm against discrimination and racism even when he received constant death threats. Jackie refused to allow those things to put fear in him or discourage him. Instead, he had a determined resolve that encouraged and emboldened him. In return for his determination, he earned the respect and support of many who believed it was time for America to finally have equal rights for all in sports. For his courage and contribution to baseball, Jackie Robinson was inducted into the Baseball Hall of Fame in 1962. Additionally, his jersey #42 was retired permanently as a symbol of honor. In this week's scripture, we see the young leader Joshua about to embark on his life journey, leading the Israelites to cross the Jordan River into the land God had given them. The journey required courage, lots of it; just as leading the Israelites who had a reputation for being rebellious and stuck in their ways. Moses, their deceased leader had led the Israelites to this point. Now, it was Joshua's turn to take the baton and lead the way into the promised land. God Himself, through His admonition put courage into Joshua, commanding him to be strong and courageous. God promises to be with Joshua all the way through the journey into the promised land and beyond. What an encouragement for educators walking in their calling as Christ's ambassadors. God Himself, has promised to be with you all the way through this school year and beyond.

Application: Is there anything putting fear in you? Honestly answer this question with at least one compass colleague.

Discussion Point: Fear is destabilizing. Faith, on the other hand, is empowering. How has your faith been stirred towards believing God? Share out loud and discuss with your colleagues.

Closing Prayer: Faithful God, thank you for your encouraging word not to be afraid or discouraged. We re-affirm our trust in You, and your command to be with us not only this school year but beyond. We declare our faith in You. We declare our hope in You. We declare our love in You.

Topic: Redeemed

Hear: Galatians 3:13 "Christ redeemed us from the curse of the law by becoming a curse for us- for it is written, "Cursed is everyone who is hanged on a tree."

Believe: Ric O'Barry is 79 years old. In his early years, Ric trained dolphins and whales for the 1960s TV series *Flipper*. After training dolphins for ten years, Ric transitioned to advocating against industries that keep dolphins in captivity. What a huge contrast from someone who used to train dolphins for a living! Ric set out on a new path after having a deep personal reflection on the cruelty of abusing dolphins and whales for human entertainment. He founded the Dolphin Project to rescue and rehabilitate dolphins around the world. Ric O'Barry successfully reclaimed the value of dolphins from being a means of entertainment to valuing their intelligence as part of creation. Ric can be said to be a "redeemer" of dolphins. Jesus Christ did the same for humanity. He is our redeemer. His death on the cross was payment for our sins and eternal separation from God. Jesus Christ became cursed for us, so that He could redeem us from the curse of the law. We were guilty and Jesus' sacrifice on the cross paid our ransom. Jesus' sacrifice bought us back and gave us access to the Heavenly Father - an access that was lost originally in the Garden of Eden by Adam and Eve. Now, everyone that accepts Jesus Christ as Savior and Lord has the seal of redemption. Hallelujah to the Lamb! We are redeemed! Educators share this redeeming quality of our Savior. From advocating for students to standing up for injustices, educators are some of the best advocates. As followers of Jesus Christ, our faith in Christ requires and empowers us to speak up and advocate for those that cannot speak up for themselves.

Application: What is the Holy Spirit saying to you through this week's study?

Discussion Point: Take some time and share with your compass colleagues what the Holy Spirit is speaking to your heart. Pray for each other.

Closing Prayer: Heavenly Father, thank you for the salvation of our souls. Jesus, thank you for taking our place on the cross. Holy Spirit, thank you for speaking truth to our hearts today. Our one desire is that you will be glorified in and through our lives. For this, we live, move and have our beings. Holy Spirit, fill us afresh with your power, inspiration, courage, and resolve to be the hands and feet of Jesus Christ – our Lord and Savior.

Topic: Unique

Hear: Psalm 139: 14 "I praise you, for I am fearfully and wonderfully made. Wonderful are your works; my soul knows it very well."

Believe: When the movie *Happy Feet* came out in 2006, it stole the hearts of both young and old. Mumble, the main character of the movie, taught us all about the beauty of uniqueness. In a community where having a singing voice is the norm, Mumble finds out he doesn't have a "heart song" (a unique song to attract a mate) like the other penguins. Instead, Mumble has a rare talent that the other penguins didn't have - tap dancing. Through a series of events marked with ridicule, rejection and disapproval from family and friends alike, Mumble comes to accept himself. He embraces his uniqueness, revels in being true to himself and changes his community for the better. This week's scripture verse highlights the truth of uniqueness. God in His intelligent design has created and wired each one of us for a unique purpose. As educators, we recognize the students that feel out of place in our classrooms or campus. Students that feel they don't belong, because they aren't part of the "cool kids" group. Students, just like Mumble, who are yet to discover who they are. The good news is God knew these students would be here on your campus and in your classroom. God knew these students would come into contact with you - a child of God. And through you, and your daily ministry in your classroom and your campus, these students will come to accept themselves and their uniqueness. The anointing of God on your life, helps call out the identity of these students. Through your words and actions, these students will embrace their "fearfully and wonderfully made" design. For such a time as this, God has brought these students to you so that they may know how God has made them unique.

Application: In what way(s) has God made you unique?

In what way(s) has God made your students unique?

In what way(s) has God made your colleagues unique? Your family unique?

Discussion Point: Briefly share with each other your uniqueness. Now, celebrate this uniqueness that expresses the beauty of our God. As you learn how to celebrate who you are, it becomes second nature to celebrate who God has created each of your students to be as well.

Closing Prayer: Heavenly Father, thank you for making us heirs of your kingdom through Christ Jesus our Lord. Help us to walk out our inheritance as sons and daughters of your kingdom.

2nd Nine Weeks Grading Period: Week 4

Topic: Helper

Hear: John 14:16 "I will ask the Father, and He will give you another Helper, who will stay with you forever."

Believe: Christmas time in America ushers in a time of giving and outreach to those in our communities that need to see a demonstration of God's love through humanity. Many cities across the nation employ the assistance of Santa's Helpers to accomplish this joyous feat. Santa's Helpers are typically people in different organizations or families that take on the task of elves; gathering toys for children and food items for families. The elves are indicative of elves that live with Santa Claus at the North Pole and help make toys that Santa distributes to those children on his "nice list." This week's scripture points us to a Helper promised to every child of God. This Helper is the third Person of the Holy Trinity - the Holy Spirit. Jesus Christ promised us a Helper that will always stay with us. This Helper ensures we are successful in what God has called and assigned us to do. The Holy Spirit is the only Person that knows each student in our classroom. With this divine discernment, the Holy Spirit can guide us in our communication with students and parents alike. He can give us creative ideas on how to deliver a difficult lesson. Because the Holy Spirit is God, we can trust His guidance. His help is readily available and all we have to do is ask Him for whatever we need help with; in our lives, students' lives, or the task of teaching. This Helper is with you always and loves to help!

Application: What do you currently need the Holy Spirit to help you with?

Is it to plan lessons creatively in a way students' will quickly understand the concepts?

Is it in how to deliver instruction in a way that targets students' maximum learning style?

Discussion Point: Briefly share with each other what you currently need help with. This could be the current challenge with a student, parent or lesson concept. Now spend some time to pray for each other, asking the help of the Holy Spirit. Commit to Him and invite Him into the challenges.

Closing Prayer: Heavenly Father, thank you for making us heirs of your kingdom through Christ Jesus our Lord. Help us to walk out our inheritance as sons and daughters of your kingdom.

Topic: Unity

Hear: Psalm 133:1 "Behold, how good and pleasant it is when brothers dwell in unity!"

Believe: Ric O'Barry is 79 years old. In his early years, Ric trained dolphins and whales for the 1960s TV series *Flipper*. The dolphin, Flipper, was depicted first by a female dolphin named Susie then by another female dolphin named Kathy and subsequently by other female dolphins named Patty, Scotty and Squirt, respectively. These five dolphins became part of a community to ensure the success of the *Flipper* TV show. Sometimes the dolphins passed as identical "Flipper." This type of synergy is what happens when there is unity. Our scripture verse points to the fact that great things happen when there is unity. To dwell together in unity requires a sense of community. It requires having the same mindset on something. This is what we want to see in our classrooms. A community of learners that share a love of learning and are actively engaged in learning from one another. To achieve this type of unity, requires dedication, focus and determination. A unified classroom means, we have standard procedures that have been duly communicated and demonstrated to students. As the leader in the classroom, we get the opportunity to set high expectations for all students in other to create a synergy of instructional excellence.

Application: How would you rate your classroom management system?
Do all students know what is expected of them daily?
Do all students know what to do in specific situations?
- Such as in a fire drill?
- Such as in a lockdown?
- Such as in a bad weather situation?
Do your students know the procedure for different tasks in the classroom?
Have all consequences, where applicable, been communicated to students?

Discussion Point: Briefly share how you have created a community of learners in your classroom with each other. Share how you may improve the classroom management system you currently have. Share what is working in your classroom with each other. Now, spend some time to pray for each other, asking for God's blessings on your classroom management systems.

Closing Prayer: Heavenly Father, thank you for our lesson this week. We want to see an increase in the sense of community in our classroom. Direct us how to ensure all our students feel a part of our classroom learning community. Thank you in advance for all you will do in each of our classes.

2nd Nine Weeks Grading Period: Week 6

Topic: Words

Hear: Psalm 19:14 "Let the words of my mouth and the meditation of my heart be acceptable in Your sight, O Lord, my strength and my redeemer."

Believe: Have you ever been caught in a situation where helping someone back fired? The result being that you become the object of disrespect through ugly acts or words? This is something many educators can relate to in the classroom or at home. This week's topic scripture verse Psalm 19:14 is a great reminder as educators when dealing with children, family, or co-workers. We must be like David who paid close attention to the words of his mouth and the meditation of his heart. David's highest goal was to ensure his words and meditations were acceptable and pleasing to the Lord-His strength and redeemer. When we align ourselves, as David did, ensuring that the words of our mouth and the meditation of our heart are acceptable and pleasing to the Lord, we show patience, gentleness, and kindness. Those who fire back are dealing with more than their miscommunication with us. There is usually a root cause that is unseen, and our words are critical especially while carrying out our calling as a Christian and a teacher. David was a man after God's own heart. He trained his mouth and heart to please God and we can do the same as educators that love the Lord and our calling.

Application: In what area do you need to ensure the words of your mouth and the meditation of your heat is acceptable and pleasing to the Lord?
Is it in your personal life?
Is it in your marriage?
Is it in your classroom?
Is it with that co-worker that just seems to push your buttons?
Is it when dealing with testing issues?
Is it when dealing with students who are not always respectful?
Is it when dealing with students who seem to push you to the limit?

Discussion Point: Briefly share some of the areas you are struggling in with each other. Prayerfully brainstorm better ways to respond to some of the issues in a godly way that will please the Lord.   Now ask God to help you respond to others in a loving and kind way.

Closing Prayer: Lord thank you for the scriptures that confirm these issues are not new nor are the answers to these issues. Help us to respond with words of love, patience and kindness so that our words will be acceptable to you our Lord. Steady our hearts as we look to you for daily strength.

2nd Nine Weeks Grading Period: Week 7

Topic: Trust

Hear: Psalm 20:7 "Some trust in chariots, and some in horses; but we will remember the name of the Lord our God."

Believe: In this week's scripture verse, it takes us back to David's time, when chariots were the greatest technology and man's input was their own understanding of how to make them faster, stronger, and safer. Compare those ancient times with the times we live in now - the speed of how we're able to get around on land, water and air. In this week's scripture, David mentions horses; which were known for their natural strength resulting in their trustworthiness. This scripture does an excellent job of reminding us to remember the name of the Lord our God and to trust in Him alone and not man. Not just in education, but in life, it is easy to put our trust in the wrong places at times. We trust in our understanding, or even the education we have, and lately we place our trust in the newest technology. We tend to forget as humans, that we are limited. Only God is unlimited, and He usually must empty us of ourselves, before He can use us. This emptying ensures our total reliance on God. It is only when we remember the name of the Lord our God and trust in Him with all our heart, that He will direct our path and use us for His glory.

Application: In what areas of your life do you need to trust the Lord and stop leaning on your own understanding?
Is it in your personal life?
Is it with your own children?
Is it in your classroom?
Is it with your students?
Is it with your colleagues?
Is it with your church family?

Discussion Point: Briefly share some areas you need to turn over to the Lord with each other. Affirm your trust in God by committing those areas to Him in prayer. Now ask God in prayer to help you lean not on your own understanding but to trust in Him with all your heart.

Closing Prayer: Abba Father, thank you for the knowledge that you have about everything in my life. No one has the knowledge needed to direct my path like You do; thank you for reminding me I can trust You when I call upon your name. I affirm my total dependence on you, my Lord.

2nd Nine Weeks Grading Period: Week 8

Topic: Serving

Hear: 1 Timothy 4:16 "Take heed to yourself and to the doctrine. Continue in them, for in doing this you will save both yourself and those who hear you."

Believe: Educators are natural givers by nature. We love to serve others and our days are filled serving our students and their parents. We know our work is vital and the Lord will not forget our work. Yes, it is important that we fulfill the calling the Lord has given us, but we cannot forget our own spiritual needs in the process. We will have nothing to share if our well is dry; with nothing left to give out. This type of state is not good stewardship. In this week's scripture verse, we can gain insight from Paul's instruction to Timothy. Timothy was the senior pastor in the world's largest church in Ephesus. He was living out the great commission of sharing the gospel. His ministry also included dealing with the many issues found in such a large congregation. Paul, his mentor and coach, cautions his brother in Christ to make sure he is paying attention to his own spiritual needs. This is the same admonition for us as educators; we must take care of our relationship with the Lord by spending time with Him. When we spend time with the Lord, our spirit is renewed, and our cup runs over. In this state, we have something to give out joyfully. When we neglect our spiritual needs, we are unable to serve others effectively.

Application: When was the last time you put your spiritual needs first?
Do you have a time set aside each day to nourish your spirit?
Do you spend some time each day in worship?
Do you take time to read God's word and meditate on it daily?
Do you spend time with colleagues in prayer each week?
Do you allow others to serve you when possible?

Discussion Point: Briefly share what you sense the Holy Spirit is teaching you from the scripture verse about stewarding your spiritual life well. Also, share some of your answers to the application questions with each other.

Closing Prayer: Thank you Father for quickening us each day to be sensitive to taking care of our relationship with you. Help us to be diligent disciples by paying close attention to meeting our spiritual needs through Your Word, worship, and fellowship with other disciples. Holy Spirit fill us in areas where we are currently depleted. Energize us by the power of our inner man so we will be strong, sharpened and prepared to serve joyfully on our campuses.

Topic: Love

Hear: Galatians 5:22 "But the fruit of the Spirit is love, joy, peace, forbearance, kindness, goodness, faithfulness."

Believe: Students in our public schools come from different walks of life, economic status and various backgrounds. Despite this, there is one thing they all have in common - their need to be loved. God demonstrated His great love for us through His action. He sent His only Son to the cross for our redemption. It was love that sent Jesus Christ to the cross to be bruised for our iniquities. And by His stipes we have been healed. In our scripture verse, we see a different kind of love - *agape love*. Agape love is the highest form of love that is sacrificial in nature. It is a supreme love that knows no limit, not even in dimensions: width, height, or depth. This love transcends time and space. We can only have, and function in, agape love through the power of the Holy Spirit. This love is ours and as Christians we are to share this sacrificial love with our students, families, co-workers, etc. Therefore, we need a consistent relationship with God to refuel our agape love tank. Only through agape love will we be able to fulfill our callings as educators and grow in the fruit of the spirit of love. What we will see flowing out of our lives is an action backed life of love to each student in our classrooms.

Application: Is there any area in your life where you are challenged to know God's love or to share God's love?
In what ways can you share God's love with your students this week?
In what ways can you share God's love with your administrators this week?
In what ways can you share God's love with your co-workers this week?

Discussion Point: Reflect on some of the areas where you are struggling to know God's agape love for you. Also, assess yourself in how you share the agape love the Lord has freely given you through the fruit of the spirit with others. Discuss your reflection and assessment with each other. Now, ask God for His help to address any area you currently feel challenged in receiving and/or sharing agape love.

Closing Prayer: Abba Father, we come to you today asking for your help in receiving and sharing your gift of agape love. Lord, we realize this is a sacrificial love and we need your grace to live this out with all our students. Fill us to overflowing with your agape love, so we can share it freely with those that need it and those that do not know your love for them yet. May they learn of your agape love through the love that we share with them. Thank you, Lord, for Your love! Amen.

Topic: Focus

Hear: Isaiah 26:3 "You will keep him in perfect peace whose mind is stayed on you because he trusts in you."

Believe: There are many circumstances and situations that can take away one's attention from helping students learn. Overcrowded classrooms, non-compliance of parents or students and behavioral issues can really affect the instructional environment. Amid it all, the focus should remain on helping students succeed. This task sometimes can be insurmountable without the help of God. He is our peace during a storm. He will help us regain our focus on what really matters. When we believe, acknowledge, trust and rely on God, He will bathe us in His perfect peace that surpasses all understanding. This is what will help us endure those hard times of teaching.

Application: What are some things you can do differently to help you stay focused?

What are those things that easily distracts you?

List at least 2 known distractors that's difficult for you to recover from and why?

Write down your answers in your journal and use it as a reflective piece when you feel distracted. Trust God for peace in your heart to help you overcome so He can be glorified. Remember, God is the same yesterday, today and forever and when you win, He's pleased. You'll never know who's watching how you respond to your distractions. Your response(s) can possibly be someone else's cure to doubt and unbelief.

Discussion Point: Briefly share with each other what does experiencing God's peace means to you.

Closing Prayer: Heavenly Father, thank you for being our Jehovah Shalom, "God of Peace." You're a loving God that wants your children to experience your fruit of peace in their lives every day. Your word promises that you will keep us in perfect peace if our minds stay focused on you. Help us God to stay focused on you in difficult circumstances and situations. Help us not to overreact and stay focused because with your help all things are possible. In Jesus' name, Amen!

Topic: Diligence

Hear: Proverbs 8:17 "I love those who love me, and those who seek me diligently will find me."

Believe: Being an educator requires hard work and patience to be successful and truly make a significant difference in students' lives. The everyday struggles of trying to teach in the chaos of systems not being in place, behavior issues, etc., really challenges every fiber of an educator's being. But, without the implementation of hard work and patience, students will not benefit if every effort is not pursued. Students don't care about how much a teacher knows, but they do need to know that you care for them. Also, that you are committed to helping them learn and grow. Trusting God enough to believe that He will reward our efforts and will help our patience mature is the foremost important element in overcoming students' weaknesses. Hence, it is important to demonstrate your love for God by diligently seeking Him as your signature for success.

Application: Do you diligently prepare for class every day or is this an area of weakness? Explain.

What does giving your all to your students mean to you?

What is your definition of diligence?

Is there someone who demonstrates diligence that you would like to emulate and why?

Record your responses in your journal for further reflection. When you seek God diligently, life becomes simplified because He will change your perspective and show you how to work smarter and not harder. He will also give you the patience necessary to not become weary while working harder even when things appear not to be changing quickly.

Discussion Point: Briefly share a time with one another that you really worked hard on something and felt like giving up but did not. Share to encourage each other what kept you from giving up?

Closing Prayer: Father God, your word says that patience has to have her perfect work and that there is profit in all labor. Father God, we need your help to be strengthened so we are not weary in well doing. Remind us of our callings when we feel like giving up and that our students' success depends on our diligence and hard work as educators. We ask and thank you for helping us stay the course. In Jesus' name, Amen!

3rd Nine Weeks Grading Period: Week 3

Topic: Action

Hear: I John 4:8 "He who does not love, does not know God, for God is love."

Believe: During the beginning of the school year, it's so easy to love all your students and colleagues as well because you're still learning them and they're still learning you. You're patient and kind to everyone. No one gets on your nerves and all your students are polite and kind to you and to one another. Fast forward to the current grading period; now you may have students that normally do well that are beginning to talk back and be disrespectful. Now these students are interrupting classroom instructions. You have conferences with parents and students but nothing seems to work at this point. Do you stoop to the level of your students and become disrespectful too? Or do you choose to act on God's word and believe what He says, "He who does not love, does not know God." Faith is believing and acting on the word of God which means not acting reactional and emotional. So, you choose to love your students.

Application: Do you react (saying and doing whatever comes to mind)?
Do you respond (apply the word of God to the situation) to chaotic situations in your classroom?
How can you demonstrate the love of God to disrespectful students?
Do you believe it's necessary to forgive to walk in love with others? If so, why?

Acting on God's word helps us to live out God honoring ways. Trust and believe that God is for you and not against you. He will show you how to love the unlovable. God wants His children to be able to do good in the presence of evil and to put His word into action, so He can get involved and turn things around for the glory of His name.

Discussion Point: Briefly share with each other a situation where you demonstrated the love of God even when it was difficult for you to. You chose to act in love instead. Encourage each other as you share those situations that challenged your love walk but you overcame by acting in love.

Closing Prayer: Heavenly Father, you are a God of love. You can never fail us because love never fails. Thank you for loving us while we were still sinners. Thank you for your continuous forgiveness of our sins. Father God you sent your Son to die on the cross for each of us to demonstrate your love for us. You saw past our failures and loved us anyway. Help us to love like you do. Help us to love our students beyond their failures. Help us to live and act out love unconditionally. In Jesus' name, Amen!

3rd Nine Weeks Grading Period: Week 4

Topic: Armor of God

Hear: Ephesians 6:10-11 "Finally, my brethren, be strong in the Lord and in the power of His might, put on the whole armor of God, that you might be able to stand against the wiles of the devil."

Believe: Professional attire is very important in our field of work. We are expected to adhere to a high standard of dressing. The way we dress oftentimes reflects how we feel about ourselves and the job. As Christians, we have a higher call for attire; which is our spiritual attire known as "The Armor of God." This is because as believers we are in a spiritual warfare and we must maintain our "battle-stance," not against co-workers, parents or students, but against satanic, unseen forces. The struggles of teaching with all the demonic forces attempting to influence us negatively are real and we must be prepared. Our defense is in putting on the whole armor of God as stated in our scripture verse. Our armor includes: Belt of Truth, Breastplate of Righteousness, Shod feet with preparation of the gospel of peace, Shield of Faith, Helmet of Salvation and the Sword of the Spirit, which is the word of God. To fasten all the pieces of our armor requires prayer that is the glue that holds the armor together. With this armor we are ready to actively engage in battle.

Application: How is your daily prayer life? Is daily prayer necessary in a Christian's life?
What are your thoughts on praying for those who might have done your wrong? Is this Biblical?
Why do you think it is important to out on the armor of God? Explain.
Write your answers in your journal and reflect on how God wants you to handle battles you encounter. We must trust the process God has mandated us to implement in order to become victorious Christians. He knows that the best way to fight darkness is not with darkness but with the word of God (Sword of the Spirit).

Discussion Point: Share with your colleagues how you currently handle struggles, disappointments and setbacks. Now share how putting on the armor of God can help you to be victorious in these situations.

Closing Prayer: Heavenly Father, thank you for reminding us to put on our armor daily. Thank you for showing us how to position our "battle-stance" against Satan's fiery darts and scheming tactics. Help us to walk in truth, righteousness, peace, faith and your word. Thank you for protecting our minds with purity and giving us hope with the Helmet of Salvation by increasing our expectations of victories in all battles. In Jesus' name, Amen!

Topic: Relationships

Hear: I Corinthians 3:10 "According to the grace of God which was given to me, as a wise master builder I laid the foundation, and another builds on it. But let each one take heed how he builds on it."

Believe: Building positive and meaningful interpersonal relationships should be a priority in every school community. The success of students should always be a major focus when building relationships. As social creatures we strive to belong and develop good friendships and relationships with positive interactions so it's imperative how and why we build them. We should intentionally strive to be our brother's keeper because what affects one affects others. God places high priority on how we treat and relate to one another. He established relationships and laid out a foundation in His word to show the necessary attributes of building caring ones. Research shows that in schools with high student achievement, caring relationships played a major role in the success of students. The same can be said about low student achievement. It takes a village to successfully help students learn and grow. Each student matters and through the building of strong, healthy relationships we can make sure that no student is left behind. Have you ever thought to ask God whom you should build a relationship with? Ask Him because He will never guide you wrong.

Application: What do you look for when establishing collegial relationships?

How important is it to you that everyone approves and like you? Explain.
Do you know of relationships that were formed that weren't for the best interest of students? Record your answers in your journal and further reflect on them as a means of checks and balances for future relationships. God is waiting for us to involve Him in our relationship building. He knows the minds and hearts of every person and knows what is best for us. Give Him a try. He will never fail you.

Discussion Point: Share with each other about a time you formed a relationship with someone and later regretted doing so? Why was this the case? Encourage each other in what to look for in building godly relationships.

Closing Prayer: Heavenly Father, show and help us with building caring and meaningful relationships that helps students succeed and bring glory to you. Father God, we are relying on you to help us stay the course and focus on what really matters - students' success. With you God all things are possible, and we know that the good work that you started in us, you will finish. In Jesus' name, Amen.

3rd Nine Weeks Grading Period: Week 6

Topic: Encouragement

Hear: Proverbs 12:25 "Anxiety in a man's heart weighs it down, but a good (encouraging) word makes it glad."

Believe: Unexpected happenings, debilitating roadblocks, and demanding duties can drain educators of the joy of influencing those within our sphere. Yet, when we are discouraged by bewildering circumstances, a simple and sincere word of encouragement can lift our focus and give us the courage and confidence to complete the tasks before us. We have a choice; to either live by our anxious feelings or to live beyond them. A timely word of encouragement helps us to live beyond the things that weigh us down, especially this time of year.

Application: Who needs a word of encouragement today in your sphere of influence?

Is that person your student? Your co-worker? Or your family member?

Who feels like a failure today? Encourage that person today.

Who received a heart-wrenching diagnosis? Encourage that person today.

Who heard a conversation that causes one to think that divorce is imminent?

Sometimes, we think that our situation is unbearable. Yet, a quick look around us confirms that everyone is burdened with things that weigh them down. Today, students carry heavier burdens than they should for their age. So, what are we to do? In our fast-paced, day-to-day activities, we should realize that it only takes a moment to speak a power-packed, thoughtful word of encouragement over a student, co-worker, or family member. Yes, it only takes a moment.

Discussion Point: Briefly share with each other about a person in your lives who uplifts your heart through thoughtful spoken words of encouragement. Pray blessings on that person. Now pray and ask God that each of you will become encouragers in your spheres of influence.

Closing Prayer: Heavenly Father, thank you for Your watchful care over us. Thank you for those around us who speak timely words of encouragement to us especially in our times of need. In return, give us Your eyes to see the disheartened who need a power-packed, thoughtful word of encouragement from us today. We ask this in Jesus name. Amen.

Topic: Praise

Hear: Psalm 150:6 "Let everything that has breath praise the Lord. Praise ye the Lord."

Believe: We are living in a time when giving thanks for everything is not even a concept to most, but it is the will of God, in Christ Jesus, for us to give thanks. Despite difficulties and hard circumstances, we can surely find reasons to thank God. Tammy is a vibrant educator that had breast cancer. Despite her situation, she had many things to thank God for like God never leaving her nor forsaking her, her church, her supporting family, encouraging friends, the peace of God through each surgery and her decision to purchase cancer insurance the year which provided more than enough money to pay for her medical expenses. Her insurance policy paid her so much money that she was able to pay off a debt on her house from a contractor who had taken $42,000 and done nothing but left a hole in her back yard. God saw her and her family through one of the darkest times of her life. Tammy was able to praise God, not for the cancer, but for all the good that came through the breast cancer. Praise exhibits our dependence on God, draws out our trust even in darkness, and shows our obedience for the One who died for us while also revealing that He now lives in us. And, one of the best reasons to praise is that when we praise, we are focused on God and not on ourselves. What we end up with for praising God despite our circumstances is joy; which in turn becomes our strength.

Application: What do you need to praise God for today despite your circumstances?
What are some things that are hindering your praise to God?
Is it your job?
Is it unanswered prayers?
Did someone get the position you wanted?
Is it in dealing with the most difficult student you have ever had?
Is it a challenging relationship with a co-worker?

Discussion Point: Take some time to discuss with your colleagues and reflect on a situation or situations that have robbed you of praising the Lord and receiving all the benefits of your praise. Follow up the discussion by praying for each other to experience God's strength and grace.

Closing Prayer: Lord help us to be thankful in all things as we trust You. Help us to trust You that you have the perfect plan for us. Create a hunger of praise in us for who You are. Lord may we praise You all the days of our lives. Lord, may we praise You and not the rocks on our behalf. Let everything that has breath praise the Lord! We praise You today, Lord!

3rd Nine Weeks Grading Period: Week 8

Topic: Proximity

Hear: James 4:8 "Draw close to God, and He will draw close to you."

Believe: In topology math, proximity is defined as the nearness of space. This week's scripture verse gives us an assurance - that if we draw close to God, He, in turn, will draw close to us. What a wonderful promise we have been given! Even though we have this great promise, the distractions of the world have left many of us distanced from God. Therefore, it is so important to schedule and guard our time with God, so the enemy does not snatch it away from us. One way to draw close to God, is through this weekly Bible Study where we get the opportunity to allow the Word of God to dwell richly in us. In so doing, the Word of God will be part of our lives, because when we do, the Word of God will enrich with spiritual wisdom and insight making us rich beyond measure. And when we are rich in our spirits, we will have an overflow of worship and counsel to freely share with those in need; especially our students who are struggling. God wants to draw close to us; but we must take the first step out of our love and desire to be with God. It is like any friendship; we want friends that want to be our friend and not a forced relationship. By drawing close to God, we are saying to Him, we want to be His friend. This divine friendship with God is spiritual wealth. Just imagine the abundant blessing of the God of the universe wanting to draw close to us.

Application: What are some things in your life that are hindering you from drawing close to God?
What are some distractions in your way of daily reading the Word of God?
Is your schedule so over booked that you do not have time to spend with God?
Do you need help in how to spend time with God?
Are you so helping others at home, school, and church that you neglect your own spiritual life?
Does your family know how important your time with God is?

Discussion Point: Take some time to discuss, share and encourage each other on practical ways to draw close to God. Share your thoughts about reading and keeping a spiritual journal to record your spiritual journey. Also share your thoughts with each other about setting spiritual goals and writing down answers to prayers as they come.

Closing Prayer: Abba Father, help and quicken us about creating a schedule for drawing close to You. Strengthen and guide us to protect our time with You. Lord we believe when we draw close to You that You will draw close to us. Create a new hunger in us to look forward to our time together. We want to be spiritually rich in wisdom, so that we may be a vessel of Your love, mercy, grace, and truth to others; especially our students and parents. In Jesus name, Amen.

3rd Nine Weeks Grading Period: Week 9

Topic: Fear

Hear: Isaiah 43:1 "But now, this is what the Lord says - He who created you, Jacob, He who formed you, Israel: "Do not fear, for I have redeemed you; I have summoned you by name; you are mine.""

Believe: Camille loves teaching and just finished her first year of teaching. As part of her summer, she had the opportunity to learn about creativity in gifted and talented (GT) students while attending a professional development conference. During the session, the presenter noted that most GT students are extremely gifted in creativity and thinking in ways that are extraordinary. However, they have experienced multiple rejections from peers or teachers in the past, which caused them to limit their own creative abilities in order to appear "normal". At this point, the Lord spoke to Camille about how she relates to GT students, even though she does not consider herself GT. She realized that fear of failure and rejection had prevented her from doing many things in life. In this week's scripture verse, the Lord is reminding us as educators, that we have nothing to fear. He also reminds us that we are not stuck in our mistakes, or in our future missteps. He does so by reminding us that He has redeemed us implying that He already has covered our failures past, present, and future. With this powerful perspective, launch out and take off the limits on yourself.

Application: Do you fear failure or making mistakes?
Do you see God as the Lord of your life; trusting that He already has gone ahead of you and has you covered?
How is God using the mistakes in your past to help your future?
How can you use a lesson from your mistakes to help your students?
Have you extended grace to students when they have made mistakes?

Discussion Point: Briefly share some situations where you have feared messing up and how the Lord worked it for your good. Encourage each other this week with Romans 8:28. Read it together.

Closing Prayer: Father, thank you for redeeming us from our failures. Thank you for giving us peace and for working out every mistake that we make for our good. Help us to look to you to be our strength and guide this week, in Jesus' name Amen.

Topic: Answer

Hear: Psalm 119: 105 "Thy word is a lamp unto my feet, and a light unto my path."

Believe: It was 4:45 AM, and Kaley had just dialed the 17-digit international telephone number and got an unfamiliar ringing tone. She tried again and again but still got the same unfamiliar tone. She knew the tone well, since her extended family lives in Chile and she typically makes international calls at least once a week. Suddenly it occurred to Kaley to re-check the number her older sister had texted her the night before. She checked the text message and to her utter surprise, it was a 16-digit number. Kaley had accidentally added another number that made the phone number 17 digits. That explained the unfamiliar ring tone she got when she dialed the number. She tried calling again, this time with the 16-digit number and the call went through. It was right at that point that the Lord began to minister to her heart about how many times we flow through life finding out things are not working as they should. However, we never stop to ask God for answers either through prayer or His word. Many times, we assume that because we have been a Christian for a while, we have all the answers. However, God will normally lead us to His word to find a scripture or story that will have the answers we are seeking. We just have to be humble enough like Kaley to re-check ourselves. God's word is a lamp to our feet and a light to our path. God has the answer; all we must do is ask.

Application: In what area of your life do you need some God answers?
Is it with a student that has been difficult to connect with?
Is it with a co-worker that you seem not to understand each other?
Is it with a parent who is proving challenging?

Discussion Point: Briefly share with each other some of the areas you are needing answers in your teaching practice. Now spend some time to pray for each other asking God for answers. Listen as the Holy Spirit speaks to you.

Closing Prayer: Thank you, Lord for leading and guiding us in your word. We ask that you light our path and understandings in those areas we are needing answers. Illuminate our hearts with your truth and give us the courage we need to follow through. In Jesus name, we pray.

Topic: Prayer

Hear: Genesis 20:17 "Then Abraham prayed to God, and God healed Abimelech, his wife, and his female servants, so they could have children."

Believe: The evidence that God answers prayer is all over the Bible in both the Old and New Testaments. The Bible hailed Abraham as a man of prayer. The essence of answered prayer is dialogue that is specific and fixed on faith in God. In our scripture verse, Abraham prayed for Abimelech and his family. God heard Abraham's prayer and healed Abimelech, his wife and maidservants so they were able to bear children. Abraham shows us what it takes to have our prayers answered by God - we must believe in God's character and ability to answer prayer. This belief in the character of God is critical to activating our faith when we come to God in prayer. The story of Hannah in 1 Samuel 1:10 is more evidence that God answers prayer. Hannah believed in the character of God and consistently poured her heart out to God in prayer. Hannah prayed with zealous faith and she received the answer to her prayer when God blessed her with a son that she dedicated to the Lord. As Christ's ambassadors in our public schools, educators can bring heaven to earth on campuses through faith-filled prayers for students and parents. The results will be noticeable as heaven permeates the hearts and minds of everyone receiving prayer. Prayer helps ensure our dependence on a faithful God. Prayer is our solid leaning wall that will never let us fall.

Application: Is there anything that inhibits your trust in God?
What do you believe about the character of God?
What prayer needs do you have for your students?
What prayer needs do you have for your family?
What prayer needs do you have for your friends?

Discussion Point: Reflect on the character of God in your life. Share this character of God with each other. This is your building block as you trust God to answer your prayer. Share prayer requests and spend some time to pray over each other's requests.

Closing Prayer: Heavenly Father, help us develop a praying heart and spirit. Teach us to pray your heart for our students, parents and community. Empower us by your Spirit to trust you for answers to our prayers. Thank you for hearing us. We thank you in advance for answers, in Jesus name.

Topic: Integrity

Hear: Proverbs 11:3 "The integrity of the upright guides them, but the unfaithful are destroyed by
their duplicity."

Believe: Public school educators are faced with many decisions throughout the school year. Schedules and the workload can be very challenging at times and difficult to keep up with. Administrators are not always watching or monitoring every step that teachers make. This is where personal integrity comes in for Christians: see yourself living out Proverbs 11:3 daily in your school. Do what is right, because it is the right thing to do and not what is easy. Integrity is everything. Integrity is doing the right thing when no one is watching. However, our heavenly Father is watching and never misses anything. He is keeping a record for that day when each Christian that has accepted His salvation and Lordship will see Him face-to-face. Doing the right thing no matter what is a form of worship to God. He longs for His children to worship Him with truth and honesty.

Application: What are some situations during this school year that challenged your honesty or integrity?
With family members? With students? With parents? With colleagues? With campus leaders? With assessment data? With daily requirements? With your special students?
To help prepare you to do the right thing no matter what, visualize these situation outcomes and how you would respond if you were honest and when you were not honest. Now record in your journal and describe how you felt knowing you did the right thing while no one was watching. The reality and truth are that, God was watching everything, and He knows our hearts. Educating students is one of the most challenging professions. However, Christians are not left helpless. God is with us every step of the way. The encouragement is that sometimes integrity means enduring short-term pain for longer term gains. Integrity is developed over time.

Discussion Point: Briefly share some of the challenging decisions you may be facing with your colleagues. See if anyone has some insight or potential solutions. Now take those challenging decisions to God in prayer together.

Closing Prayer: Heavenly Father, thank you for your love, grace, and mercies which are new every morning. We commit every decision we make to you. We are trusting you to help us increase our level of integrity and build our character. Our desire as your children is to glorify Your name.

Topic: Peace

Hear: Hebrews 12:14 "Make every effort to live in peace with everyone and to be holy; without holiness no one will see the Lord."

Believe: It is the last grading period of the school year and things get tougher with end-of-year assessments, requirements and activities. As we move farther into the school year, we are bound to face different trials, unexpected changes, relationship struggles, and struggling students. Then we have special challenges with parents and sometimes new district mandates. Things seem to go chaotic this time of year. However, as Christ's ambassadors we are peace carriers and called to be peacemakers. No matter how chaotic a situation or place may be, we have the Holy Spirit and His fruit of peace growing and expressing God's heart through us. As God's hands and feet, we must live in peace with everyone as stated in our scripture verse, despite any trials we may be facing. As peace carriers and peacemakers, we can trust and believe that God has our back. And because of this truth, we have nothing to worry or be burdened about. We can allow the peace of God to rule.

Application: What sort of trials are you currently facing?

Do you have a new administrator?

Have you just been assigned a new leadership role with extra responsibilities?

Do you have any colleague that is a first-year teacher?

Are there any new adjustments with your own family?

As you reflect on these questions, begin speaking peace into each situation. God is the only one that can give perfect peace. Trust God to handle these situations and see you through the end of the school year. Supernatural is a gift we can live in as children of God. Let God's peace rule your heart.

Discussion Point: Briefly share with each other some of the trials or struggles you might be facing this last grading period of the school year. Spend some time to pray for each other for God's peace.

Closing Prayer: Heavenly Father, thank you for taking all our struggles and trials as we are lay them down at your feet. We cast all our cares upon you, because we know you care for us. We release all our burdens to you and ask for your supernatural peace to rule and reign in our hearts, mind and souls. We lean on your faithfulness to take care of us. Thank you, for having our backs.

4th Nine Weeks Grading Period: Week 5

Topic: Endurance

Hear: Galatians 6:9 "Let not us become weary in doing good, for at the proper time we will reap a harvest if we do not give up."

Believe: As educators, we might be faced with providing support to challenging students and parents, a new team of teachers, or even the daily tasks of trying to balance work and home life. You might be thinking this is a bit much and when will it end. The feelings are valid and sometimes it looks like the finish line is so far away, especially this last grading period. However, this is not the time to quit. This is the time to activate endurance and keep going. This is when educators must have faith and continue to run the race set before us. Our scripture verse for this week shines the light on endurance. The scripture further admonishes us why we should not give up; because at the proper time we reap the harvest if we do not give up. The reward is not in the middle, it is at the end, which means we must finish and not give up. As a Christian, there is strength available to continue the race till the end of the school year, despite all the obstacles we might encounter.

Application: What is making endurance difficult for you?

Who or what is making you want to give up?

Why do you think endurance in important in our profession as well as our daily lives?

Think of an athlete and what he/she must endure in a race. As you reflect and ponder the answers to the application questions, remind yourself of your "why" and commitment to your calling and family. Remind yourself of your Savior - Jesus Christ the Son of God who endured and carried the Cross for us. During His journey He encountered many distractions and struggles. The load of the cross was heavy, but He never gave up. Jesus is our perfect example of endurance. He understands and will see you to the finish line this school year.

Discussion Point: Briefly share with each other about any hindrance you might need to get rid of, in other to run better. Now, spend some time to pray over each other for strength for the journey.

Closing Prayer: Heavenly Father, we thank you that you are a big God and there is nothing too difficult or hard for you. You see and know the long race that is before us and we ask that you help us to run with endurance. When we feel like giving up, we will remember that you have us in your hands and will help us to finish this school year strong in Jesus Name.

Topic: Patience

Hear: Colossians 3:12 "Therefore, as God's chosen people, holy and dearly loved, clothe yourselves with compassion, kindness, humility, gentleness and patience."

Believe: Our profession has many irritants that can cause daily frustration if allowed. From preparing for different events throughout the school year, results from student assessments, reluctant students, or waiting for a response from parents, the opportunities for frustration are plenty. It's in those frustrating times, that we must put to remembrance our scripture verse that admonishes us to action. These pieces of attire are just what we need to overcome the many irritants during this time of year. We need the attire of compassion, kindness, humility, gentleness and patience to combat the frustrations that come with this time of year. The best part of our scripture verse; is the fact that we are God's chosen people. That means, we are not by ourselves. As a farmer must be patient for his harvest, so we must exercise patience in dealing with end-of-school year frustrations. And we are not meant to do this alone because we have an anchor.

Application: Do you have students in your class who seem to test your patience?

What advice would you give a colleague who might be struggling with patience?

Can you see how patience is a virtue?

Do you respond to stressful situation without getting upset?

As you reflect on these questions, meditate on the scripture verse. Write down your answers in your journal. Remember that patience is waiting for something or someone without getting upset. Always think about having a positive outcome and good attitude in your time of waiting.

Discussion Point: Briefly share with each other how developing patience can make you healthier emotionally. Discuss anything during this grading period that frustrates you or tests your patience.

Closing Prayer: Heavenly Father, thank you for your loving kindness and long suffering towards us. Thank you, Holy Spirit for developing patience in us and activating our self-control when we are faced with stressful situations. We ask that You empower our inner man. We trust you to help us finish strong. We commit the remainder of the school year to you, in Jesus name.

Topic: Courage

Hear: Joshua 1:9 "Have I not commanded you? Be strong and courageous. Do not be afraid; do not be discouraged, for the Lord your God will be with you wherever you go."

Believe: In 2010, the world watched as 33 Chilean miners were rescued. These courageous men found a way to stay alive trapped hundreds of feet below the surface for 17 days before they were found. Then it took another four months after they were found before they were finally rescued. We saw firsthand the triumph of the human spirit. These men lived in great uncertainty and determined to stay alive. In a similar manner, working in education involves many uncertainties and heartaches. Educators tend to feel these unpleasantries are caused by decisions made by district or campus administrators. Take for example a position change or loss of an assistant or paraprofessional. What we must understand, as Christians, is that these decisions are not personal but simply necessary. In this week's scripture verse, God commands us to be strong and courageous which means we must determine we will finish well and not bow down to fear.

Application: What are some situations you have faced this school year that caused you to be afraid or live in fear?

How do you exhibit courage daily?

What can block courage from operating in and through your life?

Who is the source of your courage in times of uncertainty? When faced with uncertainty, the best thing to do is wait on the Lord. This seems easy, yet it is hard sometimes to wait on God. Instead of choosing fear in the face of uncertainty, choose to trust God completely. As educators we need courage to make tough decisions in our classrooms.

Discussion Point: Share with each other a time during the school year when you were faced with difficulty or intimidation. Also, discuss some of the uncertainty you might be facing as the school year ends. Celebrate all the great things each of you have done this school year. Thank God for them.

Closing Prayer: Heavenly Father, thank you that you are the God of love and peace. We trust you with everything. Thank for helping us to be bold and courageous. Thank you for the confidence of your word this week. Help us to finish this year strong and well. We turn all concerns and important decisions about the remaining school year to you. We thank you in advance, in Jesus name.

Topic: Friendship

Hear: 1 Samuel 23: 18 "The two of them made a covenant before the Lord. Then Jonathan went home, but David remained at Horesh."

Believe: The old adage of "A friend in need is a friend indeed" is a true saying. God created humans with a desire to experience true friendship. As Christians, we desire true and godly friends that can be trusted. Good friends love at all times. Many of us have high school friendships that, though we do not get to see each other often, that strong bond of friendship has lasted throughout the years. Reunions tend to validate these long-term friendships with rambunctious celebrations and excitement of seeing each other again. Our scripture verse sheds light to this type of true, loyal and godly friendship. David was running for his life due to King Saul's plan to kill him. Yet we see a strong friendship formed between Saul's son Jonathan and David. Jonathan traveled to Horesh to meet with David where he encouraged, helped David to find strength in the Lord and assured his safety. He made a covenant with David sealing their friendship. As educators we need each other and we need covenant friendships to stand strong amid our hectic schedules, workloads, demands and callings.

Application: What are some characteristics of a good friend?

Were you able to develop some new friendships this school year?

Jonathan exemplified covenant friendship with David. He was not thinking of himself though he was heir to the throne. He placed David's interest above his and wanted the best for him. This is the mark of true friendship. As Christian educators we need covenant friendships to grow and stay accountable in our calling. Covenant friendships guide us in imitating the legacy of Jesus Christ our Savior and Lord who loves unconditionally. Reflect on these types of friendships in your life.

Discussion Point: Share with each other what some of your characteristics are for a good friend. Discuss ways your friendships have been strengthened this school year. Discuss ways to cultivate covenant friendships with each other. Discuss ways to keep each other accountable even when school is out for the summer break. Share one encouraging word with each other and pray for each other.

Closing Prayer: Dear Lord, thank you for showing us through the life of Your Son, what unconditional love looks like. Because of His love for us, Jesus Christ went to the cross enduring pain, shame and suffering. Help us to be such good friends to each other. In Jesus name we pray.

Topic: Warrior

Hear: Judges 6:12 "When the angel of the Lord appeared to Gideon, he said, "The Lord is with you, mighty warrior."

Believe: At every stage of life, we see battles. As Christians we are in a spiritual battle that never ends. However, we do not battle against flesh and blood; rather our fight is against the spiritual powers of this world. Each world system is pitted against the purpose and will of God. It takes Christians who know who they are in Christ to combat these spiritual powers of the world. From our daily instruction to the growth of all our students, there is a spiritual battle to ensure we as Christian educators do not attain our goals and callings. Therefore, we must adopt the mindset of a warrior that is always prepared for battle. Since, the challenges that comes with each school day is different, we need to be ready to combat the challenges as they come. Our scripture verse reminds us that as Gideon, we are warriors in the battle of education. We are warriors in the battle for our students minds and lives. We are warriors in the battle for our schools, campuses and communities. As the Lord was with Gideon, so He is with every child of His that has committed his or her life to Jesus Christ. We do not fight alone. God is with us; this is what makes us strong, confident, courageous and bold in the face of unsurmountable challenges in our classrooms. As we close out the school year, celebrate the fact that you made it warrior educator! God celebrates you that you stood well all through the year; despite all the hardships, trials, hurts, demands and assessments. The Lord commends you, warrior educator!

Application: What are some major personal milestones to celebrate?

What are some major milestones to celebrate for your students?

What are some major milestones to celebrate for your family?

What are some major milestones to celebrate for your colleagues?

What are some major milestones to celebrate for your campus?

Discussion Point: Share with each other all the major milestones you have had individually and collectively. Discuss what made each of those celebrations as memorable. Now thank God together for keeping you through the school year! Also, spend some time in prayer for your students, parents and administrators.

Closing Prayer: Heavenly Father, we offer our gratitude and thanks for a completed school year. Thank you for helping us through each grading cycle. We give you all the praise and glory for this year!

Meet Our Authors

Dr. Johnson Obamehinti: A former Muslim, Johnson answered the call to salvation in Jesus Christ during his teenage years at an evangelistic crusade in his hometown of Ikare in Nigeria, Africa. Risking his life as the son of a well-known Muslim Cleric, Johnson was a frequent interpreter for open crusades in his hometown. His call to salvation led to his call as a missionary to America; where he had the privilege of continuing his education professionally and completing his ministerial training. As one of the few practicing African-American veterinary nutritionists in the United States; he is adept in formulating diets for over 200 species of animals and skilled in providing leadership and quality assurance services for manufacturing companies. As the author of three books, (*The Minority Homeschooler's Guide, The Power of Irresistible Prayer* and *Take Back Your Ground),* Johnson strongly believes in the demonstration of the power of God as an avenue of bringing "heaven" to earth. A frequent exceptional conference speaker, Johnson is passionate about people being saved, restored and fully equipped for their destinies. A former mentor with the *Concilio* to Dallas ISD students in disadvantaged areas, Johnson believes community impact is vital to great public schools. He is a co-founder of Oasis Focus Inc. and co-host of Oasis Connection, the TV ministry of Oasis Focus Inc. He is married to his sweetheart - Feyi, and they are blessed with three wonderful adult daughters. Johnson and his wife are active members at their local church in Southlake, TX.

Dr. Feyi Obamehinti: Feyi was born in Phoenix, Arizona and grew up in Nigeria, Africa. Though raised in a traditional Christian home, Feyi was saved at a youth camp and answered the call of God on her life as a teacher of His Word at age 15. A dynamic speaker, Bible teacher and trainer, Feyi is passionate about equipping people with the Word of Life and helping educators at all stages of their journey. As an educational expert, Feyi uses her expertise to support and provide leadership to educators at the local, state and federal levels in areas of best practices in education. She has authored four educational books (*The Minority Homeschooler's Guide, The Cooperating Teacher Handbook, Incorporating Science Apps in Grades 6-12,* and *Texas Refugee Student Framework*) to help educators in their practice. Her new Christian book, *Crushed to Restored: Principles of Restoration from the Book of Nehemiah*, provides divine wisdom from the book of Nehemiah with accompanying tools to equip Christians to confidently face any life situation with the help of the Holy Spirit. Feyi is a co-founder of Oasis Focus Inc. and co-host of Oasis Connection, the TV ministry of Oasis Focus Inc. She is married to her beloved husband - Johnson, and they are blessed with three wonderful adult daughters. Feyi and her husband are active members at their local church in Southlake, TX.

Linda Reese, M.Ed.: Linda is a native of Dundee, Mississippi and is a wife and mother of two. She is a former Dallas Police Officer and is currently a Special Education teacher at A.W. Brown Leadership Academies in Dallas, Texas. She earned a B.A. in Sociology with a minor in Psychology from the University of Central Arkansas, an M.Ed. from Indiana Wesleyan University and a graduate certificate from Dr. Frederick K.C. Price's Home Bible Study Correspondence School. She is an author, seminar and conference speaker. Her desire is to equip students for success and motivate people to discover their inherent creative power and greatness through education and the word of God and help them apply these discoveries to their everyday lives. She is also an active member of Arise Church under the leadership of Lead Pastor Chris Gutierrez in Duncanville, Texas.

Tammy Wright, M.S.: Tammy was born and raised in Fort Worth, Texas. She accepted Christ and was baptized at 11 and had a great walk with God for several years even during great dysfunction at home. Even though she believed in Jesus, her life was not a reflection of that until she started attending church, serving, going to Bible Study, and had a baby on the way at age 24. The road was long, bumpy, and hard, but with Jesus strengthening her and the Holy Spirit guiding her, she eventually became a reflection of a redeemed life. Tammy is completely sold out for the Lord. She is married with four boys from ages eleven to twenty-six years old. She is a veteran secondary Business and Marketing teacher in addition to teaching GED classes at night at a local public school. Her main goal is to love people to Jesus and to remind them, of how much He loves them every day. She is totally dependent on God and so grateful He never leaves her nor forsakes her.

Joyce Stepney Spears, M. Ed.: Joyce is a native of Opelousas, Louisiana. She is the wife of Edward Spears for 34 years, and mother of two adult children. She is a gifted educator of 25 years and currently serves as an Early Learning Instructor at A.W. Brown Leadership Academies in Dallas, Texas. She earned a B.S. in Business Management and an Education Certification from Southern University and an M.Ed. in Educational Leadership Policy and Studies from The University of Texas at Arlington. She holds both a Texas Standard Principal and Teacher Certification. She is an author, trainer, and a marketplace leader. One of her greatest desires is to provide students the best learning opportunity possible socially, emotionally and academically by motivating them to reach their greatest potential in their daily lives. She has a deep desire to build relationships with people and help spread God's word through daily interactions. She's also an active member of Trinity Church of the Assemblies of God under the Leadership of Pastor Jim Hennesy in Cedar Hill, Texas.

Vicki Vaughn, M.Ed.: Is the chief executive officer of Honorable Character; a classroom management system that utilizes Biblical principles to help teachers redirect student discipline in the classroom. Honorable Character was Vicki's first initiative when she became principal of Bethesda Christian School, where she served for thirty-three years. There she led the addition of a middle school and high school on campus and the school boasted standardized test scores in the top 10 percent of the nation for all grade levels. Honorable Character has been instrumental in creating a learning environment where students can excel. The trademarked system is in 40 states nationwide and five countries. To make the impact of Honorable Character more intentional, Vicki created a series of resources for parents to help them understand their children's learning strengths and challenges. Vaughn holds a B.F.A. from the University of Texas at Arlington and an M.Ed. from Texas Christian University.

Camille Cueto, B.A.: Camille is a native of Carrollton, Texas and she just completed her first year of teaching. She is looking forward to her second-year teaching First Grade at Stonegate Elementary in Hurst-Euless-Bedford ISD. She earned a B.A. in Elementary Education from Dallas Baptist University. One of Camille's greatest desires is to show Christ to her students daily. She hopes to make a lasting difference in the lives of her students. She also has a passion to improve the quality of education for students from low socio-economic backgrounds. She currently serves in the Altar Ministry at Gateway Church in Southlake, Texas.

The Lord's Prayer

Model Prayer From Matthew 6:9-13

This prayer is divinely rich because it incorporates all the essentials of walking with God. It is an inspiration for other types of prayers. The model prayer demonstrates the power of example as showed by the Lord Jesus Christ. He uses this model prayer to train His disciples on prayer and now the scriptures are an example for His followers on how to pray.

Matthew 6: 9 -13
Our Father in heaven,
Hallowed be Your name,
Your kingdom come,
Your will be done,
On earth as it is in heaven.
Give us today our daily bread.
And forgive us our debts,
As we also have forgiven our debtors.
And lead us not into temptation
But deliver us from the evil one
For thine is the kingdom and power
And the glory, forever. Amen.

Our Father who is in Heaven:
- Word of Adoration to our heavenly Father
- Spirit of adoption as sons and daughters of God
- Fatherhood of God- Sustainer, Provider, Nourisher, Abba, Sonship
- Personal relationship – with the living God.
- Knowledge of God's Fatherliness is revealed by the Holy Spirit

In Heaven:
- Position – Location – dwelling place.
- Heaven of heavens.

Hallow be Your Name:

- Praise, Sacred name, Awesome, Marvelous, Holy. Elohin (Supreme Creator). YHWH (Unchangeable), El Elyon (Most high), Adonai (Sovereign Ruler). Eldaah (Knowledge), El Gibbar (Mighty Warrior), Sabaoth (Host), Hosenu (Maker).

Thy kingdom come:

- Power, Kings Domain, reign and divine leadership

Thy will be done on Earth as in heaven:

- Purpose. God's will in heaven is His Glory.

God's will:

- Testament contains heavenly blessing, victory, joy, deliverance, peace etc.
- Heaven like obedience –childlike prayer.

Give us this day our daily bread:

- Dependence on God, His sufficiency –Provision. Daily mercy.
- Grace is new every morning.
- Daily request with full confidence (Ask, believe –obey).
- All freshness and fullness of our external life.

Forgive us our debts as we forgive our debtors:

- Spiritual reality; Transactional between God and us.
- Access to Father's love.
- You must forgive others to be forgiven. If you don't forgive others, you will not receive forgiveness from God.
- As food is to the body so is forgiveness to the soul.
- Test on your capacity to give – Ask God for what you can give others.

And lead us not into temptation; but deliver us from the evil one:

- Total surrender and obedience.
- Believing that the power of the Holy Spirit will keep you from the power of the evil one

For Thine is the kingdom and the power, and the glory, forever. Amen.

- Triumph and ascription of Praise to God Almighty.
- Finish with worship to Him who is the Alpha and the Omega.
- He God, is the "The Beginning, Middle and the End."

History of Public Education in America

Eleven Facts

Fact 1: The first schools in the 13 colonies opened in the 17th century. The Boston Latin School was the first public school opened in the United States, in 1635. To this day, it remains the nation's oldest public school.

Fact 2: Early public schools in the United States did not focus on academics like math or reading. Instead the schools taught the virtues of family, religion, and community as subjects.

Fact 3: Girls were usually taught how to read but not how to write in early America.

Fact 4: By the mid-19th century, academics became the sole responsibility of public schools.

Fact 5: In the South, public schools were not common during the 1600s and the early 1700s. Affluent families paid private tutors to educate their children at home.

Fact 6: Public schools in the South was not widespread until the Reconstruction Era after the American Civil War.

Fact 7: Common Schools emerged in the 18th century. These were schools that educated students of all ages in one room with one teacher. Students did not attend these schools for free. Parents paid tuition, provided housing for the school teacher, or contributed other commodities in exchange for their children being allowed to attend the school.

Fact 8: By 1900, thirty-one states had compulsory school attendance for students from ages 8-14. By 1918, every state required students to complete elementary school.

Fact 9: The idea of a progressive education, educating the child to reach his full potential and actively promoting and participating in a democratic society, began in the late 1800s. This became widespread by the 1930s. John Dewey is credited as the founder of this movement.

Fact 10: Through the 1960s, the United States had a racially segregated system of schools. This was despite the 1954 Brown vs. Board Supreme Court ruling. By the late 1970s segregated schooling in the United States was eliminated.

Fact 11: In 2001, the United States entered its current era of education accountability with the enactment of the **No Child Left Behind law**. In 2015, the **No Child Left Behind law** was replaced by the **Every Student Succeeds Act**.

Helpful Bible Study Tools

1. **Bible Background Commentary**: This Bible study tool is used to understand the cultural background of the Bible verse by verse. Each book of the Bible is explained chapter by chapter.

2. **Bible Dictionary**: This Bible study tool is designed just like an encyclopedia with articles arranged in alphabetical order. This tool is great for researching historical background and context.

3. **Bible Concordance**: This Bible study tool is great for finding cross-references, determining other places in the Bible where a word appears and for searching the meaning of the original Hebrew or Greek.

4. **Cross Referencing Bible**: This Bible contains cross references in the margins of the Bible or the footnotes.

5. **Dictionary of Biblical Imagery**: This Bible study tool is used in understanding the connotations of biblical images. This tool is used to shed light on biblical images, symbols, metaphors, motifs and figures of speech. This tool is a great companion to a Bible dictionary.

Feedback

Your feedback on this inaugural Educator's Compass is important to us. Since this is a pilot program that we intend to continue, we welcome your input as we embark on other editions of this publication. Please take a few minutes to provide us with your honest feedback. Has this weekly lunch time Bible Study been of help in your life this school year? We would love to know. **Please make copies of this feedback page for each educator to complete.** Write in the spaces provided. If you need additional space, please feel free to use your own paper. Thank you in advance for your feedback that will help guide our next edition.

Your Name: _____

Your School Name: _____

Your Grade Level: _____

Your City/State: _____

1. One of the things I have enjoyed most about this weekly lunch Bible Study is:

2. What is one major way this weekly lunch Bible Study has helped you this school year?

3. Is the current length of this study appropriate? Please explain.

4. Do you have any suggestions on improving this Educator's Compass?

Please send us your feedback forms either via email (info@oasisfocus.org) or to our mailing address below. We value your input as we move to Year 2 of this Educator's Compass Lunch Bible Study specifically for public school educators.

Oasis Focus Publishing

A Subsidiary of Oasis Focus Inc.

P.O. Box 2351

Keller, TX 76244

© 2019 ISBN: 9781074823030

Printed in the United States of America

www.oasisfocus.org

CPSIA information can be obtained
at www.ICGtesting.com
Printed in the USA
FSHW010539230719
60304FS

9 781074 823030